Possible Res. Questions : 57
59
64

Intro   ps. 92   —justify Context

Women's Leadership

Also by Carole Elliott
CRITICAL THINKING IN HUMAN RESOURCE DEVELOPMENT
(*with S. Turnbull*)

Women's Leadership

by

Valerie Stead

and

Carole Elliott

First published 2009 by
PALGRAVE MACMILLAN

Palgrave Macmillan in the UK is an imprint of Macmillan Publishers Limited, registered in England, company number 785998, of Houndmills, Basingstoke, Hampshire RG21 6XS.

Palgrave Macmillan in the US is a division of St Martin's Press LLC, 175 Fifth Avenue, New York, NY 10010.

Palgrave Macmillan is the global academic imprint of the above companies and has companies and representatives throughout the world.

Palgrave® and Macmillan® are registered trademarks in the United States, the United Kingdom, Europe and other countries

ISBN-13: 978-1-4039-9875-0   hardback

This book is printed on paper suitable for recycling and made from fully managed and sustained forest sources. Logging, pulping and manufacturing processes are expected to conform to the environmental regulations of the country of origin.

A catalogue record for this book is available from the British Library.

A catalog record for this book is available from the Library of Congress.

10   9   8   7   6   5   4   3   2   1
18 17 16 15 14 13 12 11 10 09

⌐nted and bound in Great Britain by
Antony Rowe, Chippenham and Eastbourne

Contents

Figure

Acknowledgements

This book has been developed with the help of many others. We would both like to thank the women leaders we interviewed for their time and their continued interest in our project. Their inspirational stories and optimism have encouraged us hugely in bringing this book to its fruition.

Valerie would like to thank her family for their support – Crispin, Sarah and Tom have kept me motivated throughout, and thanks to Dad for his encouragement. Carole would like to thank Tony for his encouragement and support, and Mum and Dad for their optimism in my ability to complete this project. We would both also like to give special thanks to colleagues Dr Caroline Gatrell, Dr Ellie Hamilton and Dr Elaine Swan for their continued support, friendship, reading of drafts and invaluable critical comments.

We would like to acknowledge the Northern Leadership Academy who provided funding for three of the women leaders' interviews.

This book has been informed by earlier versions of our work which appear elsewhere as follows:

Elliott, C. and Stead, V. (2008) 'Learning from Leading Women's Experience: Towards a Sociological Understanding', *Leadership* Vol. 4 (2): 159–80.

Introduction

About the book

This book is about women's leadership. It has developed as a response to some broad areas of interest. What are women's experiences of becoming leaders? How do these experiences inform how we understand leadership? What do women's experiences of becoming leaders tell us about how women learn leadership? What implications does this have for the development of women leaders? More specifically however, this book has developed as a result of one particular question. In developing our research around women's leadership, in presenting ideas at conferences, in talking to groups of students we were more often than not asked the question; why focus on *women* and leadership? While we often queried why we were asked this question when our male colleagues were not asked similar questions about their studies that focused on male leaders, we came to use this question as a keystone in our discussions. Before anyone else during our presentations could ask the question, we began to start by saying, 'why focus on *women* and leadership?' So while our short answer is 'why not' and to thereby invite discussion, our long answer is that this focus is indeed purposeful and important for the following reasons: a paucity of critical work on women's leadership; a persistent lack of equality for women in the workplace and a personal motivation to contribute to women's progression. We discuss each of these in turn below.

A paucity of critical work on women's experiences of leadership

First and foremost there is a paucity of critical work on women's experiences of leadership (Elliott and Stead, 2008; Hughes, 2000). As we explore more fully in Chapter 1, the dominant literature on leadership draws largely on studies of men (Calas and Smirich, 1996; James, 1998; Lamsa and Sintonen, 2001). A lack of critical texts examining women's experiences in the leadership literature has a domino effect of leading to a neglect of women's experiences in theorising leadership, learning leadership and leadership development (Stanford et al., 1995; Olsson, 2002; Wilson, 1995). Furthermore, where there is literature that examines women and leadership, we observe firstly a dominant focus on styles and characteristics of women leaders and secondly a greater attention paid to women leaders in business. In this book we want therefore to broaden discussion of women's leadership by focusing less on styles and characteristics and more on the relationship of women leaders and their social environment. Thus a core aim of this book is to expand our understanding of leadership as relational. Research by Morrell and Hartley (2006) into the challenges facing political leaders in local government in England and Wales, for example, talks about leadership comprising of interdependent relationships between leaders, the organisation(s) and the context. Gherardi and Poggio (2007) also note the importance of attending to leadership as 'contextualised in specific relational situations and systems' (Gherardi and Poggio, 2007: 159). In writing about leadership as relating to others, Gherardi and Poggio (2007: 159) highlight the significance of the experiences of leadership and in particular the attendant power relations with their use of the term 'relational dynamics'. In this book we want to then extend the idea of the relational through placing our research focus on women's leadership by bringing together different perspectives on the relational such as those described earlier. More specifically we want to contribute to understandings of leadership as relational through a critical examination of examples of women's accounts of their leadership experiences. Thus, we aim to explore the relational at micro levels, for example in terms of women leaders' interactions with others and at macro levels, for example in terms of women leaders' relationships with the organisation and wider social environment.

So in this book we will be asking what relations and relationships are important to women's leadership? How do these relations and relationships work, and in what ways do they influence women's leadership? In order to do this, we want to widen explorations of women's leadership beyond the business context by drawing on women leaders' accounts from a range of settings including community and the not-for-profit sectors. Furthermore, to address the lack of critical work in women's leadership research, we want to study women leaders' accounts of their leadership practice critically by exploring the impact of gender on women leaders' experiences. We also want to explore how a critical analysis of women leaders' accounts then impacts upon our conceptions of leadership. In sum, we are interested in exploring what the implications of a focus on the relational through a gender lens are in making sense of how women become and identify themselves as leaders? How does this influence how women leaders learn? And how does this then inform how we might develop leadership for women?

A persistent lack of equality for women in the workplace

A second major reason for our focus on women and leadership is that women leaders are still far from achieving equality in the workplace. The annual Sex and Power Report (The Equality and Human Rights Commission, 2008) paints a stark picture of women in positions of power and influence in the UK. They liken women's progress to that of a snail's pace, with women accounting for 11 per cent of FTSE 100 directorships and 19.3 per cent of positions in Parliament. In many cases, particularly in public service organisations such as the police, judiciary, health service and local government, they note a decline in the number of women holding top jobs. For working mothers and for women of ethnic minority the picture is even bleaker. The report observes a move from 'aspiration to frustration' as women from ethnic minorities have lesser representation in senior roles, and working mothers find the organisations' inflexibility preventing them from achieving positions of power after having children. A report on the gender pay gap, that is the inequality of pay levels between men and women, by the TUC (2008) also notes that in the UK women's work is paid less than men's with a full-time pay gap of 17.2 per cent and a part-time pay gap of 35.6 per cent. Women's lack of equality in the workplace is not unique to the UK. In the USA, The New York Times (2006) reports a continuing gender pay gap with a slowing of progress towards equal pay since the 1980s. In particular it notes the pay gap is widest among highly paid workers and that high earning jobs in areas such as finance and technology are still mostly held by men. More globally, a report of privately held international businesses in 32 countries (Grant Thornton, 2009) writes that internationally 38 per cent of businesses do not have any women in senior management roles, and that this figure remains unchanged since 2004. While some countries show a rise in the number of women in senior roles, for example

Spain, India, Sweden, Hong Kong, Taiwan and the Philippines, there are equally countries showing a decline in the number of women in senior management including the USA, New Zealand, Italy, Mexico, Russia and Poland. Each of these reports highlights a complex range of reasons for this persistent inequality including the undervaluing of women's work, women being unfairly treated in the workplace, a lack of government effort to reduce discrimination and what the UK Equality and Human Rights Commission (2008: 5) refers to as 'a persistent employment penalty for mothers'. Such statistics suggest that women have to deal with particular and persistent barriers in the workplace. The reports state that a failure to tackle such barriers does not however just concern women but is indicative more widely of a failure to develop working practices that make the most of valuable talent. A further aim for this book therefore is to take the opportunity to gain a better understanding of the barriers that women encounter through an examination of women's accounts of their leadership experience. In addition, in this book we want to explore how women experience those barriers and difficulties in their leadership practice and how they are learning to deal with them.

Personal motivation to contribute to women's progression

Our third reason for focusing on women and leadership is personal motivation. As women academics who work with theory, we are concerned that women leaders' experiences are referenced in the leadership literature and so gain more visibility. Our research with women leaders has been a particular motivation. Their experiences are so vivid, interesting and inspiring that we wanted to share them. One of our first interviewees, Baroness May Blood said, 'I am just an ordinary women with extraordinary opportunities'. However, we have found the reverse in our research, that women leaders are extraordinary both in terms of having achieved senior roles and in terms of having achieved their status with the often limited and very ordinary choices they are afforded. The work of our contemporaries has also been a personal motivation and has encouraged us to add to a broader body of work that is political and feminist, that is 'concerned with notions of progression in women's lives' (Hughes, 2002: 5). This body of work includes but is not exclusively limited to Elaine Swan's work on gender and diversity (e.g. 2006a, 2006b; also see Gatrell and Swan, 2008), Caroline Gatrell's research on working mothers and managerial roles and the maternal body (2007a, 2007b), Ellie Hamilton's study of women and family businesses (2006a); Christina Hughes' analysis of women's lives in contemporary Western societies (2002); Jackie Ford's study of leadership, identity and gender (2006; and also Ford with Learmonth and Harding, 2008). Their work has encouraged us to recognise as academics that our writing not only influences and shapes the theory and practice of leadership but also that our thinking and teaching has a responsibility to be more questioning, critical and inclusive. As feminists concerned with progression, their work has also encouraged us to think about how women are progressing and to turn our attention to how we can contribute positively to debates around women and leadership.

Therefore in summary there are good and sound reasons for a focus on women leaders. We would indeed argue that this focus is not just important but essential if studies of leadership and leadership learning and development are to reflect, more holistically, the experiences of practising leaders.

Overview of the book

This book will explore women's leadership in three ways: through an investigation of current literature which we label *Understandings of Women's Leadership* (Chapters 1 and 2); through an examination of empirical research using gender as an analytical lens which we call *Gender, Women and Leadership* (Chapters 3 and 4), and; through an analysis of implications for leadership, for leadership identity and for leadership development which we entitle *Progressing Women's Leadership* (Chapters 5 and 6).

By addressing these three areas we seek to develop arguments to challenge traditional understandings of leadership and leadership development. We also aim to develop a relational understanding of women's leadership and leadership development by exploring the accounts of women leaders' experiences. A concluding chapter, *Looking to the Future*, aims to draw together the contributions from the book, and to indicate areas for further research.

Understandings of women's leadership

Our first two chapters aim to establish why we need to debate women's leadership and how we might best approach this. These chapters will interrogate the leadership and leadership development literatures and, in what is a departure from the majority of leadership texts, review the significance of visual and metaphorical images associated with women leaders.

We conduct this exploration because we believe that our understanding of women leaders, and in particular how they become leaders, is limited by current representations – including the visual and metaphoric – of women leaders and by a dearth of empirical research.

In Chapter 1 we discuss how leadership theory continues to be dominated by men and draws largely on the white, western male experience as it occurs within mainly western hierarchical organisations. By hierarchical, we mean organisations that have clear divisions of labor across functions and according to levels of seniority. Women's experiences, we argue, are therefore largely excluded with the result that white, middle class, western male values are promoted as the norm. This stands in contrast to developing conceptions of leadership that view it as relational (e.g. Fletcher 2004; Hamilton, 2006a; Raelin, 2003), that is, as a relational practice leadership is not just concerned with the relationship between people and groups of people but also with the environment including the social context in which leadership is enacted.

Attention to visual and metaphoric representations of women leaders in Chapter 2 alerts us to stereotypical images that reaffirm associations of leadership with dominant forms of masculinity that equate leadership with the individual leader. In Chapter 2 we examine representations of women leaders as Iron Maidens, Queen Bees and Selfless Heroines and discuss the significance of the graphic images conjured by metaphors such as glass ceilings and cliffs. While these representations acknowledge the difficulties that women leaders may encounter, they nonetheless provide little in-depth critical understanding of those difficulties and the everyday life of women leaders.

With few studies addressing women's leadership experience, we argue, there remains a persistent framing of leadership and leadership development as 'gender neutral'. In other words leadership and leadership development remain broadly conceptualised with little reference to gender and the impact and effect of gender on the practice and experience of leadership. We describe how this failure to attend to gender is problematic in that it denies the experiences of those who do not fit the ideal model of leader: the white, western, middle-class male within a bounded organisation structure. We highlight that a lack of empirical research into women's experiences also means that leadership development continues to be framed by male experiences, which only serves to marginalise women's leadership practice further.

By ignoring such experiences we suggest that our understandings of leadership and leadership development can only remain limited and in conflict with current trends towards more postheroic conceptions. This leads us to challenge and question 'traditional' conceptions of leadership. How then, we ask, can we move beyond intellectual posturing of post-heroic notions of leadership as shaped by relationships with others and the environment and yet deny women's experiences and the impact of gender? How can we embrace a broader relational view of leadership while continuing to ignore gender as fundamental to shaping women's experiences of leadership? We conclude our investigation of the literature by calling for critical studies based on women's experiences of their leadership practice that would enable more in-depth understanding of what influences their practice and development as leaders.

Gender, women and leadership

In Chapters 3 and 4 we present and analyze women leaders' accounts of their experience of leadership. Chapter 3 presents empirical data from our study of nine women leaders. Here we provide our interpretation of accounts from interviews with UK women in senior roles in a variety of contexts including politics, athletics, manufacturing, further education, the not-for-profit sector, self employment and community activism. These interviewees include Baroness May Blood, Community Activist and Life Peer; Baroness Betty Boothroyd, Former Speaker of the House of Commons, President of Fight for Sight; Judith Donovan, CBE, Entrepreneur; Jackie Fisher, Chief Executive and Principal of Newcastle College; Dawn Gibbins, MBE, Entrepreneur, Founder and former Chairman of Flowcrete Group plc; Dame Tanni Grey Thompson, DBE, former Paralympian Athlete, Vice Chair of the Women's Sports and Fitness Foundation and Chair of the Commission on the Future of Women's Sport; Baroness Rennie Fritchie, DBE, Civil Service Commissioner, and; Rebecca Stephens, MBE, Mountaineer and Expedition Leader. One of our interviewees wishes to be anonymous, and we have given her the pseudonym Sayeeda Khan. She works at a senior level for a UK charitable organisation. In Chapter 4 we analyse the extent to which gender is significant in women's leadership practice. Our analysis draws on the accounts from our study, as well as other research into women's leadership, in particular work by Alice Eagly and Linda Carli (2007), Marianne Coleman (2005a, 2005b), Daniel Levinson (1996) and Susan Vinnicombe and John Bank (2003).

Chapter 3 is concerned with gathering women leaders' own reflections and interpretations of their leadership practice to help us build an understanding of how women leaders perceive and construct leadership. Our findings focus on how leading women negotiate and navigate their leadership route, revealing the public and private resources they access for support. We use their accounts to highlight the significance of a range of relationships in their becoming leaders and in their everyday practice. We propose a relational model of leadership that we call the Leadership Web. This model categorises the relationships as three overlapping interconnected spheres of influences:

- *relationship to others* in which women's experiences are framed by their relationship as a female to others including family relationships, the presence or absence of role models and mentors and the development of networks and alliances.
- *relationship to place* where women's accounts illustrate the importance of the physical locations where they practise leadership, where they were brought up and their position in society.
- *relationship to work* where women leaders' accounts illustrate barriers they encounter and also the ways in which they manoeuvre and negotiate such barriers, including the development of professional networks and alliances.

The accounts from the women leaders presented in Chapter 3 and the development of a relational understanding of leadership leads us to debate in Chapter 4, the extent to which gender is significant in the practice of women's leadership. Specifically, drawing on our study and other studies of women leaders, we analyse women's accounts through an understanding of gender as a fundamental organising practice that operates at multiple levels. We argue that gender operates at a micro level, for instance the processes of people's interactions with each other including the perceptions and expectations of how women leaders might and should behave. We also examine gender at a macro level, for example through organisational procedures and practices. We point to instances of

- the opaqueness of gendered processes where organisational processes are unclear and built upon implicit understandings of leadership as male,
- gender manoeuvres where women are filtered into particular roles and occupations that have lesser standing, and
- the importance for women of developing social capital in particular in gaining access to and membership of professional networks (Eagly and Carli, 2007)

We conclude this examination of gender, women and leadership by noting the fundamental impact of gender in the shaping of leadership. We propose that this necessarily has implications for how we conceive of leadership identity, how we understand leadership learning and how we develop women leaders.

Progressing women's leadership

Chapters 5 and 6 focus on how we might progress understandings of women's leadership and in particular how we might, through a more informed understanding, identify positive ways forward for women's leadership. In Chapter 5 we do this by exploring women's leadership identity. In particular we ask how women's leadership identity is shaped by discourse, and how such understandings might illuminate potential for change in organisational practices. Chapter 4's analysis of the impact of gender identifies that women are subject to perceptions and expectations that mean that they are not readily identified as leaders. In Chapter 5 we pursue this further by considering gender identities as a 'discursive product or effect' (Ashcraft and Mumby, 2004: 18). By taking a view of identity as produced by discourse we explore the relationship between societal narratives of gender, leadership and organisation. Drawing on examples from our study of women leaders, we structure this discussion through a framework developed by Ashcraft and Mumby (2004), that seeks to frame four differing approaches to conceptions of the relationship between discourse, gender and organisation. We go on to show how an awareness of dominant gender discourses and the power relationships associated with them afford women leaders the opportunity to perform particular leadership identities that enable them to progress. This appreciation of how women leaders understand discourses, we suggest, can provide insight into how women learn to become leaders and to influence workplace practices.

In Chapter 6 we continue our discussion on progressing women's leadership by turning our attention to how women learn leadership and how this influences how we develop women leaders. Specifically in this chapter we examine how women leaders negotiate the workplace, including dominant understandings of leadership identity, to achieve and maintain their leadership roles. We begin our examination by exploring conceptions of leadership learning as informal and as a socially situated practice. Viewing learning in this way, we argue, aligns with relational conceptions of leadership that foreground the importance of relationships with others and the social environment. We claim therefore that the everyday experience of leadership, which we identify in earlier chapters as shaped by fundamental organising practices such as gender, then becomes a rich source of learning. We go on to demonstrate however, that theories of learning pay limited attention to gender in particular. How then, we ask, might we reflect women's experiences of leadership in the theory and practice of leadership development? In response to this we draw on our findings outlined in Chapters 3 and 4 to illustrate two particular ways in which women learn leadership; the ability to recognise the impact of gender on their position as a woman leader, and; the ability for women to 'story' themselves as leaders. These interpretations enable us then to propose a workshop for the development of women leaders. We describe how this workshop rests on our findings from women leaders' accounts as summarised by The Leadership Web we introduce in Chapter 3, and how it aligns with concepts of leadership and learning as socially situated practices. Using stories as a core process we present the workshop as involving four key activities supported by input sessions and group reflection:

1. Relating Experiences – where individuals develop stories of their leadership.
2. Presenting Experiences – where individuals share their stories with other women leaders.

3. Analysing Experiences – where women leaders work with each other to reflect critically on their experiences.
4. Identifying actions – where women leaders identify and commit to actions.

We conclude this chapter by reflecting on how a call for understandings of learning and development that attend to gender and learning as a social practice offer a route for positive progression for aspiring women leaders.

Looking to the future

Our final concluding chapter presents a summary of the main contributions of this book with regard to women's leadership including implications for the fields of leadership and leadership development. In addition we propose a number of challenges for leadership research and leadership development.

Scope of the book

In this book we focus largely on research from the UK and the USA. Our study of women leaders was based in the UK, and might therefore have more resonance with women working in the UK. We have aimed to broaden our discussions by drawing on other recent studies of women leaders; notably Susan Vinnicombe and John Bank's (2003) work on Veuve Cliquot Award winners, Marianne Coleman's (2005a, 2005b) research on UK school head-teachers, Alice Eagly and Linda Carli's (2007) mainly US-based study of women leaders, Mary Hartman's (1999) collection of conversations with women leaders in the US and Daniel Levinson's (1996) study of US women's lives. We also refer to radio and newspaper interviews. The scope of this book therefore highlights for us that there is room for further published scholarly work that focuses on the experiences of women leaders more globally.

As an overview of women's leadership this book covers many important issues which indicate areas for further detailed research. For example, Avtar Brah and Jane Hoy (1989), Elaine Swan (2006a), Elaine Swan with the authors (2009) and Amy Wharton (2005) all note the interplay of gender, race and class in shaping experience. Our discussions of women leaders' accounts in Chapter 4 support this understanding. This raises questions, as posed by Swan et al. (2009) about how we might understand conceptions of leadership, leadership learning and development as classed and racialised. For instance how do race and class affect our understanding of knowledge and learning (ibid.).

We also recognise that there has been much important work on the body in the workplace. For example work by Nirmal Puwar (2004) examines race, gender and bodies and how different bodies (female and male, black and white) have different experiences and are afforded different advantages. Work by Caroline Gatrell (2007a, 2007b and 2008) examines how the maternal body is managed in the workplace and how women continue to be discriminated against because of their potential to give birth. The data that we draw on in this book points to examples of such discrimination. For example in Chapter 4, in identifying the difficulties that women face in their leadership practice. Thus, while we are able in the scope of this book to illuminate such important areas, we acknowledge that significant issues such as race, class and bodies in relation to women's leadership require further in-depth, critical examination.

Part I Understandings of Women's Leadership

1
Common Understandings: Leadership and Leadership Development

Introduction

In this chapter we have two main aims. First, we aim to highlight the limited empirical base upon which our understanding of women's leadership is formed, particularly how they *become* leading women. Second, we aim to show how conceptions of leadership and leadership development are defined from a relatively narrow research base. This chapter seeks to meet these aims by providing an overview of the major trends in leadership and leadership development research.

The lack of empirical research into women's leadership, combined with the leadership literature's tendency to draw largely on studies of male leaders in traditional organisational structures, such as business organisations and the military (e.g. work by Grint, 2005a) serves, we claim, to perpetuate an implicit understanding of leadership as a male activity that is conducted in hierarchical institutions.

Emerging from this limited empirical base is a predominantly individualistic understanding of leadership which overestimates the power and influence of the individual leader. As a result, the significance of his/her relationship with the social and organisational environment, including the role of followers, is diminished (Grint, 2005a; Kuchinke, 2005). A lack of attention to the social and organisational environment then ignores important power relations, for example, how individuals achieve leadership roles and how leaders gain organisational influence. In the management and business studies field (Sinclair and Wilson, 2002) therefore, leadership research reinforces a conception of leadership as a phenomenon that is separate from organisational values and beliefs. Standing in contrast to this view however, are a growing number of critical studies that recognise the role that values and beliefs play in shaping dominant narratives regarding the relationship between leadership and power (e.g. Ashcraft and Mumby, 2004; Ford et al., 2008; Kempster, 2009). These qualitative engagements with leadership and leadership development practice present deeper understandings of the becoming of leaders, shedding light on how leaders learn leadership and how leadership identities are shaped.

Disappointingly however, the tendency to separate individual leaders from their sociocultural contexts in leadership research is mirrored in the majority of government-sponsored surveys, reports and media profiles of successful women as referred to in our Introduction and in later chapters. This contemporary media and academic interest in publicly recognised women, or women located in work organisations, does draw attention to both their and society's attempts to understand what motivates and hinders women's success. This attention is in part symptomatic of the increasingly prominent role played by women in public life, yet simultaneously indicative of the inequalities between women's and men's pay levels and the low number of women in leadership positions, as traditionally defined. Nevertheless the lack of detailed consideration given by such surveys and profiles to the broader sociocultural structures within which women live and work limits our ability to learn how women either become successful, or alternatively, why they fail to achieve their ambitions.

We begin this chapter by examining the dominant themes in leadership literature, in particular the shift from the conception of leadership as an activity practised by individuals towards understandings that consider it to be more a process located in social activity. We then go on to explore postheroic models of leadership that position leadership as a shared and social practice. As we observe however, these understandings are remarkable for their lack of attention to women's leadership and to the significance of gender in shaping possibilities for leadership practice. We then discuss how conceptions of leadership development reflect understandings of leadership. They too therefore, largely ignore women's experiences and so gender remains an invisible influence in the leadership learning process. We then discuss how this lack of attention to women, and to gender, compromises postheroic understandings of leadership and leadership development. We conclude this chapter by asking:

- how are we to understand women's leadership?
- how are we to find alternative conceptions of leadership?
- where do we find alternatives to leadership development that include women leaders' experiences?

Dominant stories in leadership

As many writers on leadership have noted before us (e.g. Grint, 2000), the volume of leadership literature addressing the question, 'what is leadership?' is immense. It is not our intention here to review the history of leadership theory. This has already been undertaken by authors such as Bass (1990), Daft (1999), Northouse (2004), van Maurik (2001) and Yukl (2008). Rather, our interest is to study the theoretical assumptions that underpin dominant understandings of leadership. This exploration is empirically and theoretically informed. Empirically, our understanding has been influenced by our direct engagement with leading women's accounts of their experience, and indirectly through our engagement with women leaders' stories in a range of academic, practitioner and media publications. Theoretically, our approach is informed by post-structural understandings of leadership and organisation, which argue 'that reading, writing and talking are not innocent activities, but are actively productive' (Ford et al., 2008: 10). As such, we argue that to develop a deeper understanding of leadership we need to go beyond discrete organisational sites, to other locations and texts where leadership is practised and discussed. Working within this approach sensitises us to the ways in which dominant narratives of leadership find 'life' in certain texts such as film, literature and academic studies (Ashcraft and Mumby, 2004). From this perspective, understanding leadership becomes in part a process of engaging with the ways in which individuals consume, draw upon and resist leadership representations.

Taking this approach to our study of women's leadership experiences has made us aware of certain trends and themes in leadership research.

One is the dominance of the positivist epistemological position which has led many researchers to pursue a definition of leadership that can be universally applied. Researchers' attempts to prove or falsify what leadership is, has led to a focus on identifying attributes and behavioural traits associated with effective leaders. In recent years however, criticisms of this perspective have come from researchers taking a social constructionist stance, who argue that positivist perspectives on leadership are both reductionist and non-developmental (Alvesson, 1996). They advocate a move away from the search for generic individual attributes to approaches that consider leadership from a more systemic, relational perspective (Kempster, 2009).

Ford et al. (2008: 13–14) provide a succinct summary of developments in leadership theory:

> Leadership theory emerged in the trait theory of leadership which had flaws that were tackled by explorations of leadership behaviours, but the weaknesses in this approach, once identified, led to an understanding of the necessity of gaining better understanding through analysis of leadership situations. Eventually the fruitlessness of such approaches was recognised, and this led to the emergence of theories of transformational and charismatic leadership, to guru theory discourses of leadership and most recently to notions of post-heroic leadership and the leader as servant.

Ford et al. (ibid.: 17) note other categorisations of theoretical developments: a pre-1980s focus on traits, behaviours and contingency approaches succeeded by a post-1980s understanding of leadership as 'that which is concerned with the management of meaning (Smircich and Morgan, 1982) and symbolic action (Pfeffer, 1981)'.

Kempster's (2009) overview identifies three perspectives: (1) leader-centric perspectives – where research focuses on the traits, behaviours, qualities and characteristics of an individual leader; (2) follower perspectives – where researchers examine certain dimensions of leader-follower relations, including the followers' attribution of certain charismatic qualities to the leader, the influence of individual understandings of leadership and the 'romance' of leadership, that is, the view that leadership in the form of a powerful individual shapes outcomes and (3) the situational perspective. Drawing on Smircich and Morgan (1982), Kempster (2009: 43) describes the situational perspective as an understanding of leadership that sees it as a 'social process ... involving a dependency relationship in which individuals surrender their powers to interpret and define reality to others'. Theories that represent the situational perspective include Fiedler's contingency model (1967), path-goal theory (House, 1971; House and Mitchell, 1974), situational leadership (Hersey and Blanchard, 1982) and normative decision theory (Vroom and Jago, 1988). Similarly, Grint (2000) identifies three popular approaches in the conventional leadership literature: trait, contingency and situational. A fourth approach – the constitutive – calls for more grounded, qualitative studies that question the alleged objective conditions in which leaders practise. It comes from a position that views leadership as an 'interpretive affair', where leaders are active in shaping 'our interpretation of the environment' and where they also try and persuade others 'that their interpretation is both correct – and therefore the truth' (Grint, 2000: 4). In adopting a positivist philosophical orientation to arrive at definitions of successful leadership, research has, Grint (ibid.) argues, obscured rather than illuminated it as a phenomenon. The move towards research that sheds light on the social processes which shape leadership in specific contexts recognises that we all – either as leaders, followers or other interested stakeholders (including researchers) – shape understandings of the context through our actions and discursive practices (Kempster, 2009). To study the socially constructed nature of leadership therefore requires qualitative methodologies that pay attention to social practices and processes as they occur in particular contexts.

Thinking critically about leadership

Research that challenges the dominance of positivist approaches that predominantly draw on quantitative research methods for data collection are therefore working to develop more nuanced and culturally specific understandings. The assumption here is that leadership is not culture- and value-free (Adler, 1999). But as Ford et al. (2008) point out, researchers adopting a qualitative approach may be doing so in order to try and understand how to develop the quality of leaders and how leaders might become more effective.

Fletcher's (2004) analysis of so-called postheroic leadership models supports this observation. She notes that while postheroic models have the aura of democracy in the recognition that successful leadership practice is reliant upon 'social networks of influence' (Fletcher, 2004: 647), these concepts are not as inclusive as they might initially appear. Indeed, even when the role of followers is recognised, for example in the case of transformational leadership approaches, the image of the heroic leader remains as he strives to influence and motivate followers to reach their greatest potential (Northouse, 2004).

Postheroic leadership

While one of the foundation stones for postheroic models of leadership can be found in Burns's (1978) distinction between transactional and transformational forms of leadership its popularity really grew during the 1990s. Approaches categorised under the postheroic banner are distinguished by recognition of the significance of followers, and that leadership is a set of shared practices. One of the assumptions embedded in these perspectives is that everyone in the organisation should be regarded a leader, and that everyone should be given a voice is another.

Possibly the most well known of these models is the transformational approach which Northouse (2004) describes as a 'process that changes and transforms individuals', requires the leader to assess 'followers' motives, satisfying their needs ...' (p. 169) and which contrasts with transactional approaches (Burns, 1978). At a practical level transactional models – which Burns (1978) considered to constitute the majority of leadership models – translate into organisational practices that explicitly reward defined follower actions and outputs. A classic example of this is the Sales Director who awards a bonus to the organisation's top performing salesman. Leaders who adopt a transformational approach by contrast, place more emphasis on followers' needs and motives. It is a process 'whereby an individual engages with others and creates a connection that raises the level of motivation and morality in both the leader and the follower' (Northouse, 2004: 170).

When we analyse the transformational approach through a social constructionist lens we note many contradictions. At one level it chimes with popular understandings of leadership that position the individual leader at the head of the organisation leading its change and development. In this sense it would seem to have quite a lot in common with earlier trait and skill-based models. However, in recognising that leaders need to understand how followers' needs and motives can be met if transformation is to occur, leadership becomes a social process.

Shared leadership moves another step away from prevalent individualistic understandings of leadership in transformational models. Pearce and Conger (2003) argue that one of the major differences between shared leadership and traditional models is that influence is not solely conceived as a downward process, rather 'leadership is broadly distributed among a set of individuals instead of centralized in [*sic*] hands of a single individual who acts in the role of a superior' (p. 1). They attribute the interest in shared forms of leadership to a number of factors including the different ways in which work is now organised. Cross-functional teams for example, are now quite commonplace and tend to be less hierarchical. Although the team may have a team leader, she is likely to be a peer with no hierarchical authority beyond the team's activities. Another contributing factor is the speed of response that most organisations aspire to, which allows little time for delays in decision-making processes. The complexity of most jobs held by senior leaders is also cited as a factor in the move towards distributing leadership more widely across the organisation.

To summarise, we draw on Fletcher's (2004) three characteristics of postheroic models which serve to differentiate them from earlier individualistic models. These conceive leadership as:

- *Practice* – shared and distributed. Postheroic models view leadership as a shared practice. They emphasise 'collective achievement, social networks, and the importance of teamwork and shared accountability' (p. 648).
- *Social process* – interactions. The understanding of leadership here is that of an activity that is 'dynamic, multidirectional, collective' and in a continuous process of emergence (p. 649). Descriptions used to convey this as a more egalitarian form of leadership include 'servant' (Block, 1993; Greenleaf, 1977), 'quiet' (Badaracco, 2002) and 'connective' (Lipman Blumen, 1996).

- *Learning* – outcomes. Postheroic models are in part defined by their ability to create outcomes that benefit the organisation as well as individuals. Such outcomes include 'mutual learning, greater collective understanding, and ultimately positive action' (Fletcher, 2004: 649).

The dominance of the male in leadership theory

If theoretical developments – even those labelled postheroic – have not entirely been able to overcome binary understandings that separate leaders from followers, that position leaders as either villains or heroes, masculine or feminine, participative or autocratic, then discourses of leadership in society more broadly generally continue to be reinforced by 'tough, out-front, self-reliant' (Sinclair and Wilson, 2002: 1) masculine images.

In our introduction to this book we have briefly mentioned the reasons motivating us to carry out research exploring the experiences of leading women. In our own everyday and professional lives we have long been aware of the discrepancies in a range of organisational settings in the number of women considered to be leaders. Since the 1970s a significant body of literature has addressed such issues, seeking to explain why this is the case and sometimes recommending practices and policies to shift the gender imbalance. Nevertheless it was, and continues to be, our view that there have always been *leading* women; they simply lack(ed) visibility because of historical employment policies and patterns underpinned by prevailing sociocultural understandings of women's position in society.

Even in 2009 the image of the leader continues to be male, and men still outnumber women in senior organisational roles. An increasing number of studies of both contemporary women and of women in history nevertheless show us that women do occupy leading roles both within and outside the business context. Despite the focus on male political leaders ranging from Gandhi and Mandela to Hitler, Klenke's (1999) research reminds us that during the 1990s alone 13 women became presidents and prime ministers of their countries. Since then we have seen women rising to power as heads of state in countries in both the developed and developing worlds. To note just three examples, Angela Merkel became German Chancellor in 2005, in 2006 Michelle Bachelet became the President of Chile and in 2007 Cristina Fernandez became the first woman to be elected as the President of Argentina.

Yet it remains the case that women leaders' experiences and practices, particularly if they are taking place outside the business environment, are neither well documented nor analysed. Consequently, they are not incorporated in current leadership theory (Stanford et al., 1995; Olsson, 2002; Wilson, 1995). A number of authors have argued that this discrepancy exists due to the unquestioning way in which the dominant American and British literature adopt masculinity as the norm (Calas and Smircich, 1996), specifically in its white Western male form (James, 1988). A certain type of masculinity therefore dominates and this becomes seen as characteristic of leadership and management dynamics, such as the way in which formal and informal organisational decision-making processes take place. Martin (1996) notes how these are traditionally dominated by men and therefore perpetuate qualities associated with specific forms of masculinity. Dominant masculinities have also been discerned by Wacjman (1998) in terms of the managerial competencies favoured by organisations. She refers to these as action-man-type qualities: '[s]uccess means being lean, mean, aggressive and competitive' (Wacjman, 1998: 49).

This dominance of the male experience in leadership theory extends beyond the academic literature. When we examine the business and management sections of high street bookshops it quickly becomes clear that more popular conceptions of leadership draw on a very limited sector of the population. With some exceptions – for example, Gandhi, Martin Luther King, Nelson Mandela and occasionally Florence Nightingale – it is the experiences of western, white men that inform leadership research. Given that much of the leadership literature is developed by men, generally researching other men in leadership roles, it is not surprising that the focus on male leaders' experiences promotes male values as the behavioural norm (Lamsa and Sintonen, 2001).

Where – that is, the physical and material locations – research studies take place also contains a number of biases. Since the 1950s large business organisations have tended to provide the majority of research sites with, as Amanda Sinclair (2005) describes it, the great corporate leader becoming a dominant archetype. Business and management literature has effectively annexed leadership studies in recent decades. Previously, studies of leadership were more likely to have been conducted in classics and politics departments (Sinclair and Wilson, 2002). Long before this, both political and military settings have also been a rich source for leadership studies (see e.g. Grint, 2000, 2004, 2005a). Given the number of biographies and autobiographies of political, military and business leaders currently available, it would appear that leaders' profiles remain a source of interest in the media and in popular culture more widely.

Re-situating leadership

As our earlier summary of developments in leadership theory highlights, more recent situated perspectives argue that leadership is a socially constructed process. Taking this perspective encourages us to consider the significance of the choice of empirical locations and populations that have informed the development of leadership understandings. Viewing leadership as a socially constructed process leads us to focus on how leadership is embedded in and reproduced through social practices and structures including organisational and institutional cultures. It therefore lends itself to analyses of leadership at a number of levels including the sociocultural, the organisational and the individual. So, when we try to make sense of how leadership is practised organisationally we are alert to the ways in which, for example, organisational decision-making processes (for instance, recruitment, promotion and selection procedures) are based on assumptions that perceive managers and leaders as male (Wajcman, 1998). Recognising that gender is something that organisations 'do' rather than being an inherent attribute of people (Gherardi and Poggio, 2001), offers a more nuanced appreciation of individuals' leadership practice within specific organisational boundaries. Leadership as a social process therefore is one in which the identity and practice of the leader is always relational, drawing from and interacting with her social context. It moves us away from earlier leadership images and conceptions, which to a greater or lesser extent relied on the notion that the traits, skills and style of a leader could explain organisational success or failure.

Despite this move leadership is still predominantly presented, in both theory and in practice, as gender-neutral (Fletcher, 2004). In other words, the vast majority of studies do not take into account

how the rules and rituals of organisational life, and of society more
widely, create certain expectations about what leadership and leaders
look like.

Women in leadership: The significance of gender

In the introduction to this book we highlighted that the majority
of studies addressing women and leadership have concentrated on
women leaders' styles and characteristics. Alternative understandings
of women's leadership have emerged more recently however, with a
rise in the amount of leadership literature that examines theory and
practice through a gender lens. Research adopting this perspective
encourages us to argue for different models of leadership that reflect
women's experience and practice. The connective leadership model
advocated by Lipman-Blumen (2000) and the heuristic model of
leadership by Stanford et al. (1995) are examples of work that takes
this approach. A limitation of such work, however, is that it fails to
engage critically with issues of power within organisational settings.
As we have mentioned above, the dominance of masculine norms
of behaviour in the majority of organisational processes and policies might lead us to question how these models are to be practised
within such organisational frameworks. How, in other words, might
such ways of practising leadership be received in more hierarchically
organised work spaces where rigid divisions of labour apply?

In literature that more specifically addresses the significance of
gender to leadership, the tendency has been to label leadership as either
masculine or feminine in style. These more contemporary ideas about
gender and leadership assert that so-called feminine characteristics
afford women an advantage in contemporary workplaces that
favour more participative and democratic organisational styles
(Wilson, 2003). A strong claim made by these studies is that these
styles are more common among women than men (Eagly and
Johnson, 1990). Other characteristics labelled feminine that are
now deemed significant to encourage organisational change include
co-operation, openness and a caring orientation. These are qualities
that have been associated with women (e.g. Vinnicombe, 1988) and
some researchers have presented them as offering superior ways of
enacting leadership (e.g. Helgesen, 1990; Rosener, 1990). Nevertheless
there appears to be little empirical evidence to support this kind

of analysis. As Ashcraft and Mumby (2004) point out however, the connection made between women and participatory leadership (Eagly and Johannesen-Schmidt, 2001) has been challenged by other studies that suggest this can be complicated by the organisational context (Butterfield and Grinnell, 1999; Epstein, 1991; Hanson, 1996), perceptions and expectations of leaders (Carless, 1998; Staley, 1988) and ambivalence towards women as leaders (Eagly, Makhijani and Otto, 1991). Given these considerations labelling characteristics as either feminine or masculine is a moot point and gender cannot be regarded as an isolated feature of identity. Rather, gender is understood as interacting with the broader structural, social, political, historical, cultural and institutional context (Ashcraft and Mumby, 2004).

The summary, provided by Billing and Alvesson (2000) of developments in the leadership literature, argues that the qualities and characteristics traditionally associated with leadership are *decreasingly* associated with masculinity. This might ostensibly appear to be a positive trend for aspiring women leaders and those interested in women's leadership development. However, as Billing and Alvesson (2000) argue, a critical examination of these claims reveals it is more complicated than that. In labelling as feminine the skills and behaviours drawn on, for example, to execute household tasks and to rear children as transferable to leadership situations 'in a sense celebrates, the placement of women in patriarchy, i.e. as primarily responsible for children and home' (p. 150). This leads to the normalisation of women as caregivers. Billing and Alvesson (ibid.) therefore advise caution towards 'the idea that the same characteristics (feminine orientations) which earlier on could be used to disqualify women now should be the characteristics facilitating the entrance of women to, and functioning in, managerial jobs' (p. 154). Literature that presents the idea of *feminine* leadership promotes the view that female leaders are in general seen as different from male leaders. This then places women leaders in a comparative position to men leaders, or assesses them against a model of male leadership. The move in leadership studies that aims to identify feminine approaches to leadership mirrors the movement in debates in the feminist and gender literature more broadly. Earlier debates in feminist literature, for example, claimed women were no different from men and should therefore become leaders. Women, we might conclude from this, are caught in a gender trap in which they are 'constructed and reconstructed in order to make them appear suitable candidates for managerial labour' (Billing and Alvesson, 2000: 155).

Thinking critically about gender and leadership

Billing and Alvesson's (2000) observation about the decreasingly masculine nature of leadership has been particularly noted in new leadership models – even if the social processes associated with these new models are often presented as gender-neutral (Fletcher, 2004). In these models leadership is emphasised as 'a collaborative and relational process, dependent on social networks of influence' (Fletcher, 2004: 648). Fletcher further notes how the practice of leadership is considered as something to be shared and distributed throughout the organisation, creating an environment in which the positional leader is supported by 'a network of personal leadership practices distributed throughout the organization' (ibid.). The relational nature of leadership presented in postheroic models therefore works to develop a view of leadership that conceives it as a social process which is less hierarchical than earlier models. Leadership is portrayed as 'an emergent process' and 'as something that occurs in and through relationships and networks of influence' (ibid.: 649). New leadership models categorised as postheroic begin to challenge dualistic forms of analysis. They are essentially proposing a more dialectic understanding of the leader-led relationship characterised by 'multi-directional social interactions and networks of influence' (Collinson, 2005: 1422).

Even if the processes apparent in new models of leadership are not generally considered in gender terms, postheroic models mirror leader-centric perspectives in their concern to identify leadership *traits*. This, we argue, suggests a reluctance to fully accept leadership as a social process. To give an example, while traits associated with postheroic leadership might be considered feminine – 'empathy, community, vulnerability, and skills of inquiry and collaboration' – the pressure placed on women and men to '"do gender" by defining themselves in relation to these stereotypes' (Fletcher, 2004: 650) is less well examined. This, Fletcher argues, has implications for business practice. As we will explore more fully in Chapter 2, it also has implications for the ease with which women will be accepted as leaders not only in business but in society in general. If a real shift towards less leader-centric approaches is to occur then the 'belief system', the values that underpin business practice, also needs to shift. While on the one hand these new models emphasise the relational, distributed nature of leadership, on the other hand organisational reward systems on the whole demand to see evidence of individual achievement and success. The heroic leader it seems continues to attract attention. In leaders' stories of their success for example, both Beer (1999) and Khuruna (2003) note that they tend to ignore the wider social networks and relational practices that helped them achieve prominence. By way of contrast the analysis of women leaders' accounts that we present in subsequent chapters offers refreshing alternative considerations of how leadership occurs, highlighting in particular the significance of the relational at a number of levels.

Why corresponding shifts in the way work is organised have seemingly not yet occurred might be explained by the power dynamics associated with postheroic leadership models. The models more egalitarian, relational and distributed notion of leadership suggests that power is enacted 'with', not 'over', others (e.g. Helgesen, 1990). The skills and approaches needed to enact 'power with' leadership – 'such as fluid expertise, the willingness to show, and acknowledge interdependence' (Fletcher, 2004: 653) – are, rightly or otherwise, more commonly associated with powerlessness and femininity. But they could be seen more positively, for example as more flexible and fluid leadership practices. When women practice leadership in a way that enacts the skills and approaches advocated by postheroic models, this becomes especially problematic. Women's sharing of power, or their contribution to the development of others, is likely to be interpreted as the behaviour of a 'selfless giver' who 'likes helping' – behaviour which 'is likely to be conflated not only with femininity but with selfless giving and motherhood' (ibid.: 655). If women are not aware of the power and gender dynamics inherent to postheroic understandings of leadership, they may assume that drawing on behaviours categorised as feminine will enhance others' acceptance of them as leaders in contemporary organisations and so afford them greater social capital. However, as Fletcher (2004) and Billing and Alvesson (2000) suggest, because they are women displaying feminine behaviours, their leadership practice is not regarded as distinctive; they are doing what is considered 'natural' for their gender. In other words, failing to see that 'doing gender' is 'fundamentally interactional and institutional in character' (West and Zimmerman, 1987: 136) risks losing sight of how each individual might be held 'accountable' for their performance of an activity as either a man or a woman.

In summary, we might say that the continuing interpretation of personal attributes as either masculine or feminine is as prevalent in postheroic models as it is in more traditional models. The view that these are natural and innate to individuals therefore becomes reified. By focussing on leadership style the tendency to depict 'women leaders as the kind of representatives of women that follow women's "natural way of behaving", serving to reify power relations' (Lamsa and Sintonen, 2001: 257) continues. However, if we take a view of gender as a 'master identity', with inherent cultural meanings, that cuts across all situations and 'has no specific site or organizational context' (West and Zimmerman, 1987: 128), we are encouraged to analyse how roles, such as leadership, are constituted through interaction. This discursive approach therefore requires us to ask how societal narratives of gender are appropriated by individuals in certain situations, and how 'these performances preserve and/or alter the veneer of a binary gender order' (Ashcraft and Mumby, 2004: 9).

How is leadership development understood?

In this section we move from exploring the leadership literature to an examination of the literature on leadership development. In outlining the main approaches to leadership development, we specifically aim to draw attention to how such approaches mirror the tendencies of the leadership literature in their failure to take account of gender and to reflect women's experiences of becoming leaders (Bryan and Mavin, 2003; Elliott and Stead, 2008). We argue that this failure frames leadership development as 'gender neutral' and therefore sustains narrow and shallow understandings of leadership development that have limited relevance for women leaders.

Leadership development has its roots in ideas and research around leadership. However as noted by Ford and Harding (2007), in spite of a vast literature on leadership and a growing interest and investment in leadership development, there is little research concerning the core principles and underlying assumptions of leadership development.

Rickards and Clark (2006) suggest that what we mean by leadership development will be based on basic ideas of whether we believe leaders are born or made. The argument that leaders are born, they write, assumes either innate leadership, where such leaders are seen to possess particular characteristics that mark them out as leaders, or leadership that is attributed through birthright, for example, through a royal line or a political dynasty such as the Kennedy family. Rickards and Clark (2006) point out that while born leaders may benefit from development, there is an assumption that development is not a substitute for being made of the 'right stuff'. In contrast, there is a vast industry of development programmes in organisations and universities devoted to the belief that leaders can be made and therefore leadership can be developed. For instance, Ford and Harding (2007) document increasing numbers of leadership programmes in the UK public sector as a result of governmental leadership initiatives and Alimo-Metcalfe et al. (2001) note from their research in British companies that leadership development is seen as a priority.

By subscribing to the view that leadership development is worthy of examination, we are then also recognising that leadership is a matter of nurture rather than nature. This in turn assumes that we may determine how leadership is nurtured, and indicates that leadership may be conceived of in different ways. Recognising that leadership can have multiple meanings, combined with competing views on what best defines leadership does however render the issue of how leaders might best be developed as problematic (Alimo-Metcalfe and Lawler, 2001). Furthermore, an acknowledgement of leadership as something that may be nurtured or learnt draws us to an understanding of leadership that acknowledges context. Fundamental, then, to the development of leadership must be an awareness of the person, including their gender, class, race and of the relation of that person to the social, cultural, historical and political setting in which they lead.

Major themes and trends in leadership development research

Debate on how leadership might be developed focuses largely on the tension between two broad approaches: attending to the individual by taking a human capital approach and attending to the social by taking a social capital approach (Day, 2001; Hartley and Hinksman, 2003; Rodgers et al., 2003).

The human capital approach is based on an individualistic leadership model that invests power and knowledge in the individual. This model has resonance with the notion of leader as hero and whose qualities and attributes are leaderful and transferable across a range of contexts. A human capital approach is particularly visible in trait theories of leadership, as outlined in Yukl's (1999) evaluative essay on current conceptions of leadership, with its emphasis on individual characteristics and psychologised models of leadership that focus on self-understanding and personal qualities. According to Day (2001) the human capital approach works to an intrapersonal competence-based model and is therefore primarily concerned with the development of the self. Development activities might therefore privilege a focus on knowledge and skills of self-awareness, self-regulation and self-motivation.

The social capital approach can be seen as more reflective of postheroic understandings of leadership in that it attends to the relationships that a leader may have with others. For instance this might include ideas of shared and distributed leadership. Here leadership is shared among a team and is dependent upon a 'dynamic exchange' of influence among peers rather than a downward vertical leadership carried out by an individual or appointed leader (Pearce and Conger, 2003).

In contrast to a focus on the intrapersonal, the social capital approach emphasises 'using social/relational processes to help build commitments among members of a community of practice' (Iles and Preece, 2006: 324). Thus a social capital approach calls for a greater focus on an organisation's social system, with development activities emphasising awareness and social skills, such as networking, collaborative working, negotiating (Casey, 2005; Marsick and Watkins, 1997). This mirrors a rising interest in leadership as a relational concept rather than the leader as an individual and disconnected from the society in which she operates (Pedler et al., 2004; Raelin, 2003). This shift in thinking from a focus on the dependent model of individual leader as the product of a number of characteristics to leadership as a collective concern with shared potential within an organisation (West-Burnham, 2004; Pedler et al., 2004; Grint, 2005b), therefore demands a more inclusive, social and process-based focus in the theory and practice of leadership development (Gubbins and Garavan, 2005).

For example, Grint's (2005a) study of military training in the UK questioned the process of leadership as the sole agency of individuals. By highlighting four areas of dispute around leadership, he demonstrates that leadership will operate at multiple levels. He asks if it is the *person* (who leaders are), the *result* (what leaders achieve), the *position* (where leaders operate) or *process* (how leaders get things done) that makes someone a leader. Each of these understandings or any combination of them will, he argues, have implications for leadership development.

Raelin's (2003) concept of leaderful practice has resonance with models of distributed and shared leadership in that he views leadership as dynamic and invested in different people at different times. His work suggests a collective rather than an individual sense of leadership leading to development activities that emphasise collaboration rather than control.

However, leadership as a relational practice is not just concerned with the relationship between individuals and collections of individuals but also with the context, including the social, political, historical and cultural climate in which leadership is enacted. The literature indicates an increasing interest in the role of context in shaping leadership and therefore leadership development (Alimo-Metcalfe and Lawler, 2001; Pedler et al., 2004). The importance of this is particularly acknowledged within the public sector (Hartley and Hinksman, 2003; Finger and Buergin Brand, 1999) where multiple stakeholders, public accountability and multiagency working demand more flexible models of understanding and performing leadership.

By viewing leadership as relational, that is connected to and drawing from the social context in which it is enacted, leadership development must necessarily be more inclusive in its approach. This shift in emphasis takes us from the development of leaders to the development of leadership as embracing leaders, followers, their interactions and their interplay with their social, cultural and political setting. Leadership development must then seek to address the social role of leaders by attending to networks, relationships and resources within the leader's social setting (Hosking, 1997; Gubbins and Garavan, 2005). However, while theoretical debates acknowledge multiple views of leadership, paying attention to the social, calling for more inclusivity and with greater focus on the way in which the leader is shaped by and influences her site of practice, there is still a stubborn persistence in the literature to ignore issues of gender (Roan and Rooney, 2006). This theoretical exclusivity then has implications for how we develop leaders.

Leadership development and women leaders

As noted by Day (2001), Iles and Preece (2006) and Rodgers (2003) leadership development appears to be in conflict between the development of the individual (leader development) and the need to attend to collective leadership capacity (leadership development). Therefore while leadership theory recognises a shift towards a more relational, collectivist view of development, as Iles and Preece (2006) note, many development models continue to favour the use of competency models, psychometric testing, emotional intelligence frameworks and behavioural models that have a particular focus on the individual in isolation of their social context. In this next section we explore leader and leadership development and the implications of different approaches for the development of women leaders.

Leader development models

Leader development models focus typically on the development of the individual with little reference to context. Adair's action-centred leadership approach for example, places its emphasis on developing the leader's authority through knowledge (1989). Van Velsor et al. (1998) place the individual at the heart of leadership development with a focus on the assessment of the individual to identify particular characteristics that can be developed. A further example is Boyatzis (1982) and Boyatzis et al.'s (2002) development model based on three clusters of competence that seeks to support individuals to achieve leadership through focusing on actual and ideal self images.

Alimo-Metcalfe and Alban-Metcalfe's (2001, 2005) leadership diagnostic model drawn from questionnaires to over 2000 managers in the UK public sector provides an example of behaviour-led development.

In this model ideas and practice are developed contingent on circumstance. Their model emerged from individual (including women, black and minority ethnic BME) leaders' descriptions of behaviours that they attribute to leadership. As a result they propose dimensions of transformational leadership that are based around key areas of leading and developing others, personal qualities and leading the organisation. This model seeks to provide a developmental framework that is more culturally sensitive to the leaders of the UK, and places its focus on the aspirational rather than on practice. Thus their behavioural dimensions list a number of qualities and attributes that leaders need to aspire to. For example, in their scales measured by the Transformational Leadership Questionnaire (Alimo-Metcalfe and Alban-Metcalfe, 2005: 66), being decisive is annotated as 'decisive when required; prepared to take difficult decisions and risks when appropriate'. The focus is on perceptions of the ideal leader, on what leaders 'should' do rather than what they 'do' do. In this way, contingency, being able to read the right circumstances in which to behave, rather than the social, cultural and historical context, is foregrounded.

These examples of developmental models emphasise the leader as a sum of particular behaviours, competences and characteristics. Leadership, within this kind of approach is seen less as a social practice drawing on the leaders' relationship with others and their environment but more as an accumulation of particular skills and attributes. A lack of attention to the social interactions and practices of leadership presents an assumption of a gender-blind context, that men and women face the same challenges. Research into women and leadership however shows that women face particular barriers. For example, Burke and Vinnicombe (2006) note a range of barriers including male stereotyping, preconceptions and exclusion from corporate networks. With an assumption that the workplace is a neutral environment, developmental approaches that do not attend to a leader's social environment can then exclude women leaders by not addressing the particular difficulties they may face. With a lack of attention to context, individual leader development models offer limited insight into the 'how' of leadership, for example, how leadership is achieved within a particular organisation or how decisions are made within a specific workplace. This, in turn limits our understanding of gender to behaviours and characteristics. Wajcman

(1998) notes that leadership attributes are invariably seen as masculine, for example, being tough, being assertive. Such leader development models in their focus on behaviours and styles of leading can disadvantage the woman leader by favouring the male as the ideal aspirational leader.

Leadership development models

Iles and Preece (2006) in their review of leadership development assert that leadership development should not be conflated with leader development. Leadership models focus rather on the building of relationships and social networks which enables, Iles and Preece observe, 'an appreciation of the social and political context and its implications for leadership styles and actions' (2006: 325).

Examples of leadership development might then include those models that place a focus on organisational development rather than personal development. As such they reflect the importance given to models of shared and distributed leadership (such as Pearce and Conger, 2003; Muijs and Harris, 2003). Heifetz and Linsky (2002), for example, use the idea of adaptive leadership, that is, working with organisational change situations to help develop leaders and the social capital they require in their practice. A further example is the systems psychodynamic model by James and Arroba (2005) which focuses on the dynamics of the leadership role in the interaction between the personal, individual and the organisational. Models that place their primary focus on the organisational can however preclude the diversity of sites in which leadership is enacted. For example, typically women have had a long history of leadership in community and home-based settings (Hartman, 1999). An organisational emphasis can also reflect a particular traditional, hierarchical and therefore masculine notion of what it is to be a leader.

More recent work has shown however, an emergence of development approaches based on experience that aim to mirror the shift towards relational ideas of leadership and to work across boundaries. Kempster (2009) for example, argues for experience-based development in his study profiling directors' learning from experience. Day's review (2001) offers a detailed analysis of leadership development with attention to a range of processes involving engaging with experience, such as use of job assignments and action learning.

Pedler et al. (2004) promote leadership as active, situational, contextual and relational. With a focus on the 'connected' individual rather than the 'heroic' individual, they see leadership development as assessing situations, acting on them and learning from them. Their leadership development text outlines core leadership practices and comprises a series of leadership challenges working with and through others based on the core theme of interdependence. A further example is provided by an interest in the authenticity of leaders (e.g. see Avolio et al., 2004) which places greater emphasis on leaders' values and the extent to which others identify with those values. This in turn has led to an interest in how authentic leaders might be developed and a focus on values has necessarily indicated a more relational approach. For example, how might leaders convey values to others? (Eagly, 2005a). Shamir and Eilam's (2005) work for instance, suggests a range of developmental interventions based on life stories including identifying important events and guided reflection on challenges.

While some of this work flags up the need to attend to gender (notably Day, 2001 and Kempster's acknowledgement that his study is based on men's experiences 2009), there are few development approaches that specifically address the significance of gender. Important exceptions include Gherardi and Poggio's work (2007) that describes the use of narrative in leadership workshops for women and Eagly's study (2005a) that explores gender in the development of authentic leaders. Gherardi and Poggio (2007: 160) argue for a reflexive approach to leadership in order to enable women to challenge what they call 'the traditional paradigms of "objectivity" and "detachment" that support "the dominant models of knowing in organizations and producing knowledge on organizations"'. Eagly (2005a) draws on experiences of women to demonstrate how it is more difficult for women to be identified as authentic. She highlights, for example, that women have a 'legitimacy deficit', that is, women leaders are not attributed the same authority as male leaders (ibid.: 470). These studies indicate that for women leadership is different in that their experiences in their relationships with others and with their workplaces are different than the experiences of men leaders. Women therefore have different leadership development requirements. Such approaches are however the exception rather than the rule. Indeed, our review of leadership development suggests that there is a significant gap in critical studies based on empirical research of women's experiences that address women's leadership development.

With men viewed as the 'natural inhabitants' of the organisational domain while women are 'out of place' (Ford, 2006: 81), perhaps it is not altogether surprising that leadership development largely reflects a gendered stance. Gabriel (2005), for example, notes that many leadership programmes within business schools and universities are based on masculine principles that maintain a gendered view of leadership 'leaning heavily on game and military metaphors' (p. 158).

Consideration of gender is however timely and significant to leadership development. Burke and Vinnicombe (2006: 8), for instance, observe how organisations 'lament the shortage of leaders' and yet continue to limit women's career horizons. UK and international reports (Equality and Human Rights Commission in the UK, 2008; and Grant Thornton International Business Report, 2009) demonstrate that in spite of more women in professional and managerial positions, pay and power remain unequal. Gatrell and Swan (2008) show that in spite of increasing legislation around gender, organisations continue to ignore issues of gender. Leadership development therefore, in its continued construction as 'gender neutral' serves only to maintain such biases.

Conclusions: Leadership and leadership development

Although recognising that women's leadership experiences may be different, our exploration of common understandings of leadership and leadership development draws attention to the literature's predominant focus on leaders' styles and characteristics. Leadership research and research on women's leadership more specifically, continues to address leadership as separate from the broader sociocultural structures within which it takes place. Studies that adopt more qualitative methodologies by contrast recognise power relationships inherent to leadership, recognising it as a social process in which both leaders and followers are dependent on each other. Analyses undertaken from a discursive perspective view leadership as a process that is subject to constant interpretation and re-interpretation. In this sense leadership is in part a process of persuasion, of leaders' attempts to convince followers that their interpretation and approach are correct. Nevertheless leader-centric perspectives remain the norm and the search continues to define what characterises successful leaders. In recent years, the literature has heralded feminine characteristics and ways of working as important, yet theory and practice continue to adopt masculine values that reify existing power relations as the norm. Writing about women and leadership appears to sustain a picture of women enabling rather than enacting leadership, and so the status quo of the heroic individual male leader remains.

Leadership development necessarily draws on the particular leadership principles and theories that underpin it. While showing signs of movement towards a more relational understanding, leadership development theorising and practice continue to mirror many of the tendencies inherent in the leadership literature, in particular its lack of attention to gender. A lack of attention to women's experiences in the leadership literature, coupled with a view of gender as a marginal or non-issue leads, we argue, to a framing of leadership development as gender neutral. The continued exclusion of women and the sustained lack of focus on gender, renders problematic the move to postheroic understandings of leadership and leadership development. So, while leadership and leadership development research maintains a focus on bounded hierarchical organisational settings, it occludes broader conceptions and fields of practice. Leadership developmental approaches therefore remain stuck within a specific organisational frame. Broadening the research base to include other experiences and to take account of different sites of practice encourages recognition not only of other types of leadership that don't fit the masculine hierarchical norm, but also of the interplay between the leader and the broader social setting in which they practice. This encourages consideration of the ways in which fundamental issues such as gender, class and race inflect leadership conceptualisation and practice. This in turn, we argue, will promote approaches that attend to the social (Day, 2001) and are concerned with *leadership* rather than leader development.

Given that women leaders' experiences feature little in leadership and leadership development theory, our focus in Chapter 2 is to examine common representations of women's leadership that do exist. We do so in order to work towards understanding some of the practices that influence common understandings of women's leadership. In our analysis we include visual as well as verbal images to deepen our understanding of perceptions of women's leadership in the broader sociocultural context including how women leaders' identity is represented in the media and popular culture.

2
Visualising Women's Leadership: Stereotypes and Metaphors

> We all create images of things we fear or glorify.
>
> —(Gilman, 1985: 15)

In Chapter 1 we discussed how in spite of growing numbers of women in leading positions and leadership roles, much of the leadership and leadership development literature largely fails to reflect women's experience and practice of leadership. Chapter 1 highlighted that much of the literature is based on studies of men leaders in hierarchical organisations. We argued that as a result of this narrow research base, dominant ideas and approaches to leadership continue to promote individualised and gendered conceptions that ignore women's experience. Furthermore, we argued that approaches to leadership development mirror the predominant tendencies in the leadership literature and take little account of gender. Approaches are therefore presented as 'gender neutral', that is leadership and leadership development are promoted as being unaffected by gender (Acker, 1995). Yet, as Wajcman (1995) and Swan (2006a) argue, leadership development theorising and practice continues to promote individualistic, largely masculine and heroic understandings of leadership. In this chapter we turn our attention to the depiction of women's leadership. We are especially interested in bringing attention to a hitherto relatively little explored area, namely what do images of women leaders – be these visual images (e.g. photographs or pictures) or verbal images (e.g. metaphors and stereotypes) – reveal to us about women's leadership as a social, cultural and political phenomenon? How does this frame our understanding of women becoming leaders and of women's practice of leadership? In the spirit of Ashcraft and

Mumby's (2004) feminist communicology of organisation, our aim is to examine 'the dialectical tensions between mundane micro-level social practices' – such as the use of verbal imagery (Mitchell, 1984) in the form of metaphors and stereotypes – and 'macro-level institutional processes of reproduction and transformation' (Ashcraft and Mumby 2004: 115) in discussions of women's leadership.

In this chapter we move our debate forwards in three key ways. First, we note that in spite of women's experience and practice of leadership being largely excluded in mainstream literature, there is nonetheless a great deal of interest in women leaders. We begin by examining this interest, in particular by discussing the ways in which women leaders and women's leadership are represented across a number of sites including the media and popular culture. We are interested in unpacking the significance of images associated with visual metaphors and stereotypes including 'glass ceiling', 'Queen Bee' and 'Iron Maiden'. What, we ask, can the images conjured by this verbal imagery tell us about women's leadership in contemporary society?

We begin by examining what are viewed as invisible barriers to women's success – 'glass ceilings', 'glass walls' and 'glass cliffs'. In particular we discuss the extent to which such metaphors help or hinder women's achievements and how they can exclude more detailed considerations of women leaders' workplace context. We then go on to explore in more detail three stereotypical ways in which women leaders are categorised. These include the way in which women are portrayed as having to be like – or tougher than – men (e.g. Queen Bee, Iron Maiden) and how the ideal woman leader can also be positioned as one who surrenders herself in the name of the greater good (Selfless Heroine). Drawing on gender frameworks, we debate some of the implications and effects arising from the use of metaphors – which conceptualise women's leadership experiences in such narrow and stereotypical ways – for understanding and positioning women as leaders. We illustrate how little acknowledgement is paid to the social, political and cultural context and the gendered nature of organisation and work that impacts upon women's leadership experience and practice. We pay particular attention in our discussion to the role images play in communicating particular representations and consider their relationship to the broader sociocultural landscape. Leadership images, we argue, are social representations and therefore 'complex sites of social interaction and struggle over meaning' (Guthey et al., 2008: 4). We suggest that the use of leadership collocates such as perception, image, metaphor and representation implies 'an unarticulated theory of pictorial representation' and that this theory 'influences the way that researchers 'see' leaders, followers, and organizations ...' (ibid.).

We conclude this chapter by arguing that understanding perceptions of women's leadership requires an exploration of the broader social landscape in which it takes place. Developing an awareness of the influence of prevalent leadership representations on understandings of what constitutes successful leadership creates a more nuanced appreciation of the particular challenges faced by women leaders.

Imagining metaphors and stereotypes

In developing a framework for understanding visual images of organisational leadership Guthey et al. (2008) alert us to the fixation in organisation and leadership studies with 'mental or verbal images to the exclusion of visual ones' (p. 8). The widespread use of terms such as 'image', 'picture' and 'perception' implies, they suggest, 'an unarticulated theory of pictorial representation and its relation to mental and verbal imagery' (p. 4). Morgan in his work on 'Images of Organization' (1983), for example, does not consider an image to be an observable object. Instead, images become a 'way of seeing', an 'interpretive construct' or a 'metaphor' (Guthey et al., 2008). When analyses of photographs have occurred, in corporate annual reports for example (Dougherty and Kunda, 1991; Anderson and Imperia, 1992), they have not sought to investigate the more profound 'ideological and constitutive roles such images can play' (Guthey and Jackson, 2005: 1063). In critiquing the social constructionist leadership literature's narrow understanding of images as 'social representations' they argue that 'if representations are indeed social, then they are not only collective, but also relational and interactive' and that leadership images must therefore be considered as 'complex sites of social interaction over struggle and meaning' (Guthey et al., 2008: 5). One man's amusing image of a female political leader we might say, is one woman's prejudicial image reflecting socially accepted visions of leadership.

Our intention in examining the visual imagery conjured by metaphors and stereotypes associated with women's leadership is to offer an alternative understanding of the relationship between seemingly mundane micro level social practices – such as the unquestioning use of metaphors and stereotypes to describe and represent women's leadership – and macro level institutional reproduction and transformation processes (Ashcraft and Mumby, 2004). These include the ways in which gender is reproduced in organisations by formal and informal organisational decision-making processes such as recruitment, and promotion and selection procedures that are based on assumptions which perceive managers and leaders as male (Wajcman, 1998). We begin by examining the images of 'glass ceilings', 'glass walls' and 'glass cliffs'.

Representing 'invisible' barriers to success: Glass ceilings, glass walls and glass cliffs

Over the last few decades there have been many attempts by academic researchers, the media and government agencies to explain why the number of women in leadership positions within organisations remains relatively low. Among gender scholars the glass ceiling – sometimes referred to as the glass wall (Eriksson-Zetterquist and Styhre, 2008) – has become a popular metaphor to describe the variety of barriers that prevent women from reaching the highest levels of authority within government, parliament and organisations in a variety of sectors. According to Debra Meyerson and Joyce Fletcher (2000), as a metaphor the glass ceiling represents the degree to which gender discrimination has been embedded in organisations. The variety of studies that examine the notion of the glass ceiling on the whole recognise that the number of women working in positions of higher authority across a variety of sectors has increased substantially from the 1960s. Davidson and Cooper (1992) for example, cite US figures that show women's employment figures moving from 30 per cent in 1950 to 45 per cent in the mid-1980s. Similarly, the latest UK figures indicate that there are approximately 13.6 million women in the workforce (5.72 million of whom work part-time), while 16.06 million men are in employment (1.77 million of whom work part-time) (National Statistics Office, July 2008). Nevertheless despite women's increasing participation in the workforce, evidence that the glass ceiling remains a metaphor worthy of empirical investigation comes through recent surveys by the Equality and Human Rights Commission, and Cranfield School of Management's 'Female FTSE100 Report' through which we learn that in 2007 women only occupied 10 per cent of the Directorship positions in FTSE100 companies. According to the Equality and Human Rights Commission, if current progress in promoting equal opportunities in organisations (particularly those in the private sector) persists, then it will take women 65 years to achieve parity in the Boardroom. The Equality and Human Rights Commission's report suggests that in the UK public sector the pace of change is even slower. Currently, only 20 per cent of women are MPs and it will take another 195 years to reach equality. Among the judiciary, it won't be until 2067 that the number of women judges will match the number of men. Within councils the situation is even worse, with the Equality and Human Rights Commission predicting that women will never reach equality unless more action is taken.

Even if the metaphor of the glass ceiling has become a well established phenomenon, supported by evidence demonstrating that women face more career barriers than men (Simpson and Altman, 2000), not all researchers find it a useful way to make sense of the problem. Raewyn Connell (2006) argues that the glass ceiling approach understands gender as 'two fixed categories of persons – men and women – defined by biology' (p. 838) and that this 'categorical' approach to the understanding of gender is insufficient. Gender, she suggests, is a 'dynamic system, not a fixed dichotomy' (ibid.), and the gendering of organisations concerns 'patterns of interactions and relationship' (ibid.) that stand above differences – perceived or otherwise – between individuals. These interactions, we suggest, also include recourse to certain stereotypes to describe women leaders – a group of individuals who constitute a minority in senior organisational positions and who are thus 'other' to the male leadership norm.

More recently, the term 'glass cliffs' (Ryan and Haslam, 2005; 2007) has been coined to frame what Ryan and Haslam identify as a 'second wave' (2007: 550) of discrimination that women face in the workplace. In response to Connell's observations on the limited explanatory potential of the glass ceilings metaphor, the metaphor of glass cliffs is an attempt to convey a more nuanced appreciation and understanding of the barriers facing women practising leadership. In particular, it has been put forward as a response to commentators such as Elizabeth Judge (2003: 21), who argues that 'the triumphant march of women into the country's boardrooms has ... wreaked havoc on companies' performance and share prices'. With the image of the glass cliff, there is an acknowledgement that more women than ever are reaching higher level management positions, but that they are often appointed to leadership roles associated with a greater degree of risk. Ryan and Haslam (2005) examined the performance data of FTSE100 companies with the highest percentage of women directors. They observed that in the months leading up to the appointment of women directors these companies had consistently performed poorly. They argue (Ryan and Haslam, 2007: 556):

> [W]omen were more likely than men to be placed in positions *already associated* with poor company performance. Because of the likelihood of continuing poor company performance in these circumstances (subsequently borne out), female directors, thus, were more likely than male directors to find themselves on a glass cliff. That is, their positions of leadership were more risky and precarious (i.e. at greater risk of being associated with failure) than those in which men found themselves (emphasis in original).

Research provides evidence for the existence of glass cliffs, and in its recognition of the significance of context moves us away from more individualistic gender frameworks. However, as Ryan and Haslam (2007) acknowledge, it fails to explain why it is that women are more likely to be placed in more precarious leadership positions. Reasons for this may, they suggest, reflect implicit theories of leadership where 'women are seen as better suited to crisis management than men' (p. 557), which in turn reflect beliefs that 'women are best equipped to deal with the socioemotional challenges that (potential) crises present' (ibid.). But they acknowledge that other social, psychological and social structural factors may also have a role to play in the existence of the glass cliffs phenomenon.

Connell's (2006) critique of the glass ceiling metaphor hints at the degree to which visual imagery can reify existing social gender dynamics. By adopting a relational approach that conceives the study of gender more as a pattern of social relations, we are better positioned to ask what, or whose, 'interests and values are served through the communicative construction of certain (gendered) realities and identities, and in what ways does this construction process limit agentic possibilities for certain groups' (Ashcraft and Mumby, 2004: 129). Ashcraft and Mumby do not look specifically at the role images play in the development of their analytic framework. However the benefit of paying attention to the role the mental imagery of metaphors and stereotypes performs in the formation of leadership identities is that it makes us more alert to how these identities are formed across many sites including the media and popular culture. What do these mental images symbolise about women's chances of attaining senior roles, and to what extent do they reflect prevailing beliefs about women's position in organisations?

Stereotypical images of women leaders

> Stereotypes arise when self-integration is threatened. They are therefore part of our way of dealing with the instabilities of our perception of the world.
>
> (Gilman, 1985: 18)

In his work on the strength of stereotypes Gilman argues that they arise from our anxieties about the world and project images that bear little critical scrutiny. They permeate all areas of society including literature and popular culture, so it is perhaps not surprising that when we examine representations of women leaders, they tend to conform to a narrow range of images. Given the dominance of the white, western male experience in leadership research that we have documented in the previous chapter it may seem somewhat paradoxical then to note a fascination among the media and academic researchers with the subject of women leaders over the last couple of decades. For example, in the UK context we noted above reports from public agencies such as the Equality and Human Rights Opportunities Commission that highlight women's lower earnings in comparison to men. We also observe national newspapers providing lists of powerful women (e.g. the rise of female head teachers in the UK, The Independent, 2008; the 13 most powerful Muslim women in Britain, The Times 2009), and the business press provides annual lists of Britain's most powerful women (e.g. Management Today, 2006). This interest however is in itself contradictory and highlights a dissonance between theory and practice. On the one hand the media and academic literature depict women's success in leadership, yet on the other hand they indicate the difficulties for women in achieving senior positions of authority. While theory promotes leadership models applauding the benefit of 'feminine' characteristics, practice shows that embracing the feminine affords women less leadership capital than men (Billing and Alvesson, 2000; Fletcher, 2004; Swan, 2006a). An examination of the simplistic and stereotypical ways in which women leaders are represented in the media and the literature highlights this dissonance, as does the corresponding dearth of visual images (photographs, portraits, statues) documenting women's leadership (Gatrell, 2008), let alone its success. To do this we examine three stereotypes of women in leadership roles: Queen Bee, Iron Maiden and Selfless Heroine, which position them as the 'other', or what Judi Marshall (1994) refers to as 'travellers in a male world', and whose characteristics are defined in relation to the dominant male managerial group. This look at stereotypes has relevance in exploring women's leadership in multiple ways. According to Gilman (1985) stereotypes are 'a crude set of mental representations of the world' that 'perpetuate a needed sense of difference between "the self" and "the object" which becomes the "Other"' (pp. 17–18). His psycho-analytic analysis of stereotypes' role in shaping history and culture asserts that our creation of stereotypes cannot be separated from how human beings become individuals. They arise when 'self-integration is threatened' (p. 18) and constitute one way in which we deal with challenges to our perception of the world. Stereotyping is a 'universal means of coping with anxieties engendered by our inability to control the world' (p. 12) and draws on a set of images for the 'Other' that 'are the product of history and of a culture that perpetuates them' (p. 20). In other words they cannot be separated from the historical context. This does not mean that we have to accept them. Mitchell (2005) refers to stereotypes as living images due to the space they occupy between fantasy and technical reality forming a "mask" or a "veil" that stands between people. That they can become taken for granted is through their near invisibility, 'insinuating themselves into everyday life' (p. 296), and are at their most effective when they remain:

> unseen, unconscious, disavowed, a lurking suspicion always waiting to be confirmed by a fresh perception. The confirmation of the

> stereotype is thus usually accompanied by the disclaimer "I have nothing against ..., but ...", or "I am not racist, but ...". (ibid.); the prejudicial images conjured by stereotypes can take on a life of their own 'in the rituals of the racist (or sexist) encounter.
>
> (p. 297)

Stereotypes therefore draw our attention to the sexist way in which women leaders are depicted. On the one hand, as we go on to explain, they demean and trivialize women's achievements, but on the other hand they also reveal gendered systems and practices that are important to address. They illustrate implicit theories about leadership and gender and general perceptions regarding the perceived incompatibility between views on what it is to be a leader and what it is to be female (Ryan and Haslam, 2007).

A critique of stereotypes concerning women leaders therefore is, we believe, long overdue. Like Wajcman (1995), we too are uncomfortable with debates about women's leadership that draw on stereotypes which occlude and exclude the range and depth of women's experiences of leadership. We take Kray and Thompson's (2005) view that such stereotypes are based on belief systems that not only presume to represent how men and women act, but also to represent how they are expected to act. Schein's (1973, 1975) examination of stereotypes of managers, of men, of women and the relationships between these stereotypes demonstrates that both male and female managers regard men as more likely to possess the characteristics that lead to being a successful manager. As Ryan and Haslam (2007) note, subsequent studies replicating Schein's work (Deal, 1998; Eagly, 2005b; Schein, 2001) illustrate the durability of these views, particularly among males, regarding the relationship between what constitutes managerial and what constitutes male. While these studies go some way to explain the ubiquity of certain stereotypical images of women leaders, we are weary of being continually confronted by this range of shallow and one-dimensional representations of women. Nevertheless examining such stereotypes draws attention to the effects of their use and how they serve to perpetuate prejudice and marginalisation.

For example, Hamilton (2006a) in her study of family businesses highlights how role types given to women in family businesses maintains their invisibility as agents of influence because the boundary between their paid and unpaid work becomes blurred. So while women may be equal partners in determining the direction of the business, for instance, they are not necessarily given a public title that makes that contribution visible. Broadbridge and Hearn (2008), in their consideration of research into gender and management, highlight that gender stereotypes play a significant role in preventing women from developing their careers. In the following sections we explore three stereotypes of women leaders in-depth; Queen Bee, Iron Maiden and Selfless Heroine.

Queen bee

Mavin (2008) claims that the Queen Bee metaphor is used to describe senior women who fail to help and support one another:

> The 'Queen Bee' is commonly constructed as a bitch who stings other women if her power is threatened and, as a concept, the Queen Bee blames individual women for *not supporting* other women.
>
> (S75)

The label of Queen Bee was first used in the 1970s including the work of Staines et al. (1973), to explore women's attitudes towards women's liberation. Queen Bees, they contended, were women who felt they had achieved success without women's liberation and who were therefore of the opinion that if they could do it why couldn't others. Abramson (1975) used the term Queen Bee to label women who were in senior roles and refuted the existence of sexual discrimination in the workplace. These women, she argued, felt that the acknowledgement of sexual inequality would belittle their achievement. Mavin (2006a) claims that a resurgence of the term in the popular press is used as a way of describing women who behave in unsupportive ways to other senior women if their position is at risk. Her study offers an array of examples from popular texts, such as Dellasega's book (2005) that explores women's aggression towards each other and suggests coping strategies to press articles that construct women in negative and derogatory terms. One such example is *The Independent on Sunday* article by Sarler (2008) that talks about 'Fleet Street's bitch goddesses', the female columnists or 'Wednesday witches', she writes, 'from whom no woman is safe'.

The Queen Bee label, Mavin claims (2008), puts women in a difficult position. Mavin (2006a, 2008) argues that by vilifying women who do not support each other, women are then placed under unrealistic expectations of sisterhood and solidarity in *having* to support one another by acting as role models, mentors and career coaches. Why, she asks, do we 'continue to negatively label women as Queen Bees while holding expectations of solidarity behaviour from senior women that we can't fulfil?' (2008: S76).

While many women freely acknowledge barriers to the advancement of women into senior roles, Mavin claims that they do not necessarily want to lead or 'take the mantle of responsibility' (Mavin 2006b: 349) for advancing other women. This doesn't render them as Queen Bees, but when interpreted from an individualist (Wharton, 2005) perspective on gender, can force them into a position of defence, of not doing the right thing, of not being a sister. Their stance might be interpreted as standing in contrast to calls for women's networks as a means to achieve organisational equality. Citing reports by the Equal Opportunities Commission (Miller and Neathey, 2002), Demos (McCarthy, 2004) and Opportunity Now (Vinnicombe et al., 2004), Perriton (2006) suggests that many women have taken the lead provided by these reports and joined women's networks to meet other females occupying similar, or more senior organisational positions with the aim of progressing their careers. Despite the encouragement of the EOC, Demos and others however, it seems that there is little empirical evidence to support the idea that women's networks do lead to progression to more senior ranks. Drawing on research by Brass (1985) and Ibarra (1992), Perriton (2006) suggests that while women are not necessarily 'wasting their time in participating in women's networks, their time might be more beneficially spent developing greater ties to their (white) male colleagues' (p. 107). Davies-Netzley's (1998) study of the perceptions of women in corporate positions on corporate mobility seems to support this view. The women interviewed by Davies-Netzley speak of the difficulty of penetrating 'old boys' networks, with one woman speaking of the need to network with senior men if women are to reach powerful positions:

> The power is still in the males 50-plus years old. If you want to reach the top, those are the people you have to network with.
>
> (p. 347)

Davies-Netzley argues that the views of the women in her study echo those in Moore (1988), who argues that even when women have achieved senior positions they continue to be 'outsiders on the inside' (ibid.), often perceiving themselves as 'invisible' among their senior male colleagues.

These and other studies that take account of the socially constructed nature of organisational relations, emphasise Mavin's (2006a) suggestion that the continued use of the label Queen Bee as an unproblematic term fails to take into account complex organisational gendered systems and practices. They challenge individualistic, trait theories of leadership which assume that successful leaders hold certain individual qualities and characteristics that encourage a 'blame or fix the women' position (Mavin, 2006a: 271), where women are dammed if they do and dammed if they don't. The irony of stereotyping the perceived behaviour of some women leaders with the Queen Bee analogy is that research into bee behaviour indicates that in the natural world the queen does not control the hive; an assumption underpinning what is deemed to be their 'unsisterly' approach. Rather her sole function is to act as the reproducer to ensure the survival of the hive; she is 'simply an egg-laying machine' (www.britishbee.org).

Iron maiden

The Iron Maiden as stereotype depicts the women leader as someone who takes on and displays masculine characteristics and traits in her practice of leadership. The popular representation of Margaret Thatcher, former Prime Minister of the UK from 1979–90, provides a stark example of this stereotype.

As a public figure and an internationally recognisable woman leader she was famously know as the Iron Lady. Frequently depicted in the press as more masculine than her male political colleagues, images of her as a leader included severe headmistress-type caricatures to sado-masochistic images of her brandishing a whip. Attention was drawn to her perceived desire for control, her low voice, her strictness, her assertiveness and her aggressiveness. Her representation in the media exaggerated what was regarded as her 'manliness' and mocked her femininity. Caricatures displayed her as exploiting traditional female qualities in manipulative ways such as pretending to be caring of male colleagues while at the same time demeaning male members of her

Cabinet who were often shown as small, cowering and insignificant in her presence. The use of such derogatory and sexist cartoons was employed to illustrate that not only is it ridiculous, laughable, inappropriate and improper for women leaders to take on 'masculine' characteristics, but also that women are unable to do this in a way that is 'leaderful'. Therefore, images of Margaret Thatcher displayed her assertion as aggression, her determination as being scary and her focus as being forceful. In an interview with Margaret Thatcher's son Mark about his mother, Cockerell (2008) asks why, against all odds, he felt that his mother had managed to break through the glass ceiling to become Britain's first woman prime minister. Sir Mark Thatcher's response: 'My perspective as her son is very straightforward – she was the best man for the job', suggests that only by displaying masculine traits and qualities could she aspire to such a position. In her review of a documentary entitled 'Reputations: Florence Nightingale – Iron Maiden', Salvage (2001: 172) observes parallels between the media treatment of Margaret Thatcher and historians' treatment of Florence Nightingale, who was labelled with derogatory terms such as 'control freak, religious maniac, and repressed lesbian – hysterical, power crazed, deceitful, manipulative and cruel'. Like criticisms of Margaret Thatcher, she notes that criticism of Florence Nightingale is similarly sexist with a push to change her image from 'angel' denoted by what Salvage calls 'sticky-sweet submissiveness and self sacrifice' to 'harridan', neither of which reflect, she asserts, the complexity of her leadership or her achievement in dealing with patriarchal systems and structures. In this way the Iron Maiden stereotype can be viewed as a reinforcement of the gender binary, that is, the way in which male and female and masculinity and femininity are represented as polar opposites (Knights and Kerfoot, 2004). The woman leader as Iron Maiden is not interacting in a way that is appropriate to her gender and thus is found wanting. This results, as demonstrated by the examples of the images of Florence Nightingale and Margaret Thatcher, in enduring caricatures that not only render the women as poor imitations of men but also serve to fix femininity as something that is inherently not suited to leadership.

Selfless heroine

The notion of Selfless Heroine who places other needs beyond her own desire for personal fulfilment is widely depicted in the media.

One interesting example of this – particularly in view of the small number of portrayals of ethnic minority women leaders in popular literature and the media – is the way in which the story of Pocahontas is depicted by Disney. Dundes (2001) examines the Disney story of Pocahontas as an idealised modern heroine and role model for young women. The Disney story of Pocahontas is based on a real person, a young woman who leads her community to stand up for its rights against English settlers in the early 18th century. Pocahontas has been hailed as breaking the traditional Disney role model of submissive women waiting to be rescued in order to live happily after. As one of the few heroines whose story doesn't end in matrimony, Pocahontas was promoted as a young woman leader, an independent adventurer led by passion and values. Analyses of Disney heroines by Henke et al. (1996), for example, position Pocahontas as an important change in Disney's treatment of women, where her ambition directs her choices rather than her notions of romantic fulfilment. However in spite of images of the young Pocahontas braving physical danger and being the one to rescue rather than be rescued, Dundes (2001) reveals a character that is ultimately based on deep-rooted gender stereotypes of selfless sacrifice and altruism. At the closing sequence of the film, and contrary to the life story of the real Pocahontas, the Disney Pocahontas puts duty before her desires by staying with her community rather than travelling to England. This triumph of selflessness over selfishness, Dundes argues, sustains a stereotype of women leaders as self-sacrificing and duty-bound, prepared to put themselves before others and to give up their own ambition for the greater good. This stereotype of selfless heroine is an image that is associated with characteristics of motherhood. Women are thus represented or viewed as selfless givers who enjoy helping and expect little in return.

Fletcher contends:

> women often experience being expected to teach, enable, and empower others without getting anything in return, expected to work interdependently while others do not adopt a similar stance, expected to work mutually in non-mutual situations, and expected to practice less hierarchical forms of interacting even in traditionally hierarchical contexts.

> (2004: 655)

Such expectations lead to women being equated with caregivers (Elliott and Stead, 2008). Women leaders viewed as selfless heroines are then in danger of being exploited. What might be viewed as leadership roles such as enabling and empowering others might then be seen as natural to women and therefore not noteworthy of reward or leadership status.

Implications and consequences

Implications arising from the articulation of such stereotypical images, alongside the framing of women's leadership as a difficult journey that requires the negotiation of glass ceilings and glass cliffs, are multi-layered. In this next section we review the consequences and implications of this kind of imagery with regard to the positioning of women leaders and the understanding of women's leadership. We must nevertheless acknowledge that there are positive aspects to such representations. After all, discussions and debates referring to images of glass ceilings and glass cliffs foreground the difficulties that women face in achieving positions of leadership. They highlight the unique aspects that women bring to leadership roles and bring to our attention the low number of women leaders in the workplace; if we had gender equity we would be less likely to hear of Queen Bees (Gatrell and Cooper, 2007). Through images depicting the Selfless Heroine we can appreciate positive aspects of 'feminine' leadership such as empathy. Furthermore, women are illuminated as being tough/resolute and capable/focussed (Iron Maiden). The implications arising from these images we suggest are significant in that they simultaneously reveal social interpretations of how women do leadership and highlight the very different experiences that women leaders encounter as well as the difficulties they face in being accepted as equally valid as men leaders. However, the chief utility of such images – and the everyday, taken-for-granted way in which they are articulated – is that they encapsulate, portray and communicate important issues of gender that reflect wider social discourses.

Taking a view of gender that operates in different ways and at a number of levels enables us to examine the effects of such stereotypes in more detail. We develop our analysis of gender operating at multiple levels, based on work by Wharton (2005), further in Chapter 4 in a discussion of women leaders' accounts of their experiences.

In this chapter we use this understanding of gender operating at multiple levels in particular to examine the effects and implications of stereotypical images of women leaders and women's leadership. The effects and implications of such images can become particularly powerful when they appear in the media as the visual imagery conjured by these stereotypes communicates certain expectations about the performances from, and identities of, women leaders. They – and the particular publications they appear in – are of themselves, 'products of interaction between a variety of corporate and cultural intermediaries pursuing different interests' (Guthey et al., 2008: 29).

One level at which gender might be understood, for example, is as residing in personalities, characteristics and attributes. Wharton (2005) describes this as gender operating at an individual level. In this kind of analysis men and women are depicted according to particular traits, for instance men are viewed as determined and women are seen as enabling. While men are seen to be advantaged if they take on female qualities (Swan, 2006a), women who appear to seek to take on masculine qualities – as represented by the Iron Maiden stereotype – are not similarly advantaged. Rather, as Knights and Kerfoot (2004) note, displaying masculine qualities can be highly problematic for women. This may serve to reinforce male domination through use of masculine behaviours to assert leadership, or it may reinforce the gender binary as women risk being labelled as untrue to their gender by not displaying qualities associated with femininity.

Women leaders portrayed as Selfless Heroines might also be considered in relation to women who put postheroic leadership approaches into practice (Fletcher, 2004). Enacting postheroic leadership practices such as sharing power and developing environments that enable collective learning are, she argues, relational practices that are conflated with femininity and associated with the selflessness of mothering. This raises difficulties for women leaders and for the development of postheroic practice in a number of ways. First, the gender expectation that women behave in a selfless way can render their leadership practice invisible as they are, after all, 'doing what they always do'. Men however, undertaking relational leadership practice may be recognised as trying something new. Fletcher (2004) goes on to suggest that this association of the postheroic with mothering renders the reciprocity of relational practice invisible or makes it 'disappear' (p. 655). Therefore, the very principles upon which notions of postheroic leadership are based – the interaction and mutuality of engagement and empowerment – are constrained in their social attribution to either men or women. Thus men in enacting such principles may be seen to be doing leadership while women enacting such principles may be viewed as just doing what is natural to women.

However, taking a view of gender as a 'master identity' with cultural meanings, which cuts across all situations, and 'has no specific site or organizational context' (West and Zimmerman, 1987: 128) encourages an analysis of how roles, such as leadership are constituted through interaction. Taking this approach alerts us to where and how men and women interact in a way that is seen as appropriate to their gender, how they 'do' gender (Wharton, 2005). The image of women in leadership as Selfless Heroine might then be seen as appropriate in that selfless giving is seen as 'doing' (feminine) gender. Images of women leaders as Queen Bees or Iron Maidens are, on the other hand, highly disruptive as women are not interacting in an appropriate way; they are not 'doing gender'. Queen Bees viewed as selfish and ambitious do not 'do' gender in their ambition to achieve and their perceived lack of selflessness in not supporting other women. Iron Maidens do not 'do' gender in that they seek to play men at their own game by employing masculine traits in their leadership practice and in their interactions with men. Stereotypes of women leaders therefore may either disrupt or confirm particular constructions. By assigning women leaders to such stereotypes women in leadership roles, West and Zimmerman (2005) argue, are often assessed as 'out of place' (p. 77), as they are operating outside the narrow range of what is deemed appropriate behaviour for their sex. The image of a woman dressed in traditional male office attire brandishing a whip serves to highlight her otherness. The effects of such assessment result in a reinforcement of a view that considers women leaders as unnatural inhabitants of leadership roles, unless they interact in ways that are viewed as traditionally feminine which of themselves are not seen as leaderful. This then, has the effect of maintaining the view of women as different and deficient (Wajcman, 1998: 54).

Gender might also be understood as embedded in and reproduced through social practices and structures and organisational and institutional cultures (Wharton, 2005). Wajcman asserts that 'the dominant symbolism of corporations is suffused with masculine images', therefore ideas of success equate to being 'tough, forceful leaders' (1998: 49). Her study demonstrates how gender is reproduced in the workplace by formal and informal organisational decision-making processes (e.g. recruitment and promotion procedures) that are based on assumptions which perceive managers and leaders as male.

These ideas raise issues with regard to how we understand and view women's leadership and women's development as leaders. With work and organisational life dominated by masculine archetypes, the notion of glass ceilings and glass cliffs can have the effect of keeping women from achieving positions of leadership. They have to be tougher, work harder, overcome more obstacles and prove themselves more capable than their male counterparts. While many women leaders would recognise this as akin to their experience we suggest that we need more positive representations and images that reflect women's leadership experiences in a deeper, more nuanced way. These might include representations that highlight the strategies that women leaders employ, and the resources women leaders can draw upon, in their leadership practice.

The more prevalent negative stereotypes draw attention to the lack of acknowledgement given to the complexity of women in leadership roles. For instance, Fletcher (2004) argues that stereotypical representations are commonly presented in isolation of the gendered schema, that is, they ignore the social identity (sex, race, class, organisational role) of the leader, and the social setting (the social, cultural, historical and organisational environment) in which women are practising leadership. While we would contend that some representations are very pointed in their reference to social identity and setting, such as the example of Margaret Thatcher as Iron Lady, such representations are nonetheless broad generalisations. As an instance of verbal imagery that conjures the vision of a woman in man's clothing, the suggestion is that only a man – or at a stretch, a woman who acts like a man – can lead a nation.

In addition to having a clearer understanding of the sociocultural conditions in which leadership is practiced, we contend that we also need to find more sophisticated understandings that reflect more accurately the complex nature of the context in which *women* practice leadership. The lack of norms for women as leaders promote the understanding of leaders as men with associated 'male' characteristics (Indvik and Northouse, 2003; Mavin, 2006a; Wharton 2005). Hughes observes that women are thus in a position of having 'to negotiate their femininity and sexuality' (2002: 41). This leads to a no-win situation for women in leadership roles. Should they display feminine characteristics which do not fit the perceived leader norm? However, if they show masculine characteristics they do not fit the perceived female gender role which defers to male authority (Powell and Butterfield, 2003: 92). Continuing to promote women in leadership as a negative construct, these stereotypes sustain the positive leadership norm as masculine and individualistic. Knights and Kerfoot (2004) argue that the discourse that maintains representation of women as 'other' sustains women in a subordinate position to men. Documenting women's experiences of leadership and taking a more critical and embedded view of women's leadership will, we argue, enable us to move beyond simplistic stereotypes to a deeper understanding of women leading.

Concluding summary

We began this chapter by noting the paradox within the media and academic's interest in women's leadership. The chapter has suggested that a fascination with women leaders, coupled with the dearth of in-depth studies examining women practising leadership, results in individualistic interpretations of women's leadership that tend towards the stereotypical. Through a critical exploration of the Queen Bee, Iron Maiden and Selfless Heroine stereotypes – including the visual images conjured up by such stereotypes – we have drawn attention to how they illustrate the durability of beliefs that associate being a leader with being male. We discussed how, in assigning women leaders to such stereotypes, women in leadership roles are often assessed as 'out of place' (West and Zimmerman, 2005: 77), as they are operating outside the narrow range of what is deemed appropriate female behaviour. Women leaders are therefore seen as unnatural inhabitants of the leadership role, as 'travellers in a male world' (Marshall, 1984), unless they interact in ways that are viewed as traditionally feminine, which by themselves are not seen as leaderful.

Our analysis of how women leaders are represented leads us to call for more in-depth and critical studies of women leaders. Specifically we note a gap in understandings of women leaders in relation to the social context of their leadership, and a need to develop and broaden the research base of women's leadership. This leads us to question: what are women's experiences of becoming leaders, and what influences their leadership practice and their learning of leadership? We seek to address these questions in Chapter 3. In so doing we aim to shift discussions of women and leadership away from the stereotypical towards a more nuanced view of how women lead, and what enables or hinders them in their leadership practice.

PS 57

what strategies do they employ
and what resources do they
call upon in their leadership
practice

do they believe that gender matter

Part II Gender, Women and Leadership

3
Women's Experiences of Becoming Leaders

[D]on't forget if you are coming into a political party in here you have worked with that party for many years and you are known nationally, and therefore you have friends here and therefore your friends would be helpful. I mean you don't come into the House of Commons at an election not knowing anybody because you obviously – I am talking about the Labour Party because I know that best – you obviously have worked in the Labour Party for many years, you have been to party conferences, you know people here and therefore you have got a friend – they might not be a very close friend – but at least you have got somebody who knows which is always very helpful.

—Baroness Betty Boothroyd, first woman Speaker of the House of Commons

This quotation from our interview with Baroness Betty Boothroyd, first woman Speaker of the House of Commons highlights the theme of this chapter: what are women's experiences of becoming leaders? In this quotation Betty Boothroyd indicates that becoming an MP is not something that is done in isolation. In this account she describes the context to this achievement as the culmination of different experiences, and she also points out that there are relationships that support this role including contact with others. We concluded the previous chapter by proposing that we need more critical studies to explore women's experiences of leading, so that we can gain a deeper insight into what enables women to become leaders. In this chapter therefore, we want to examine women's accounts of their experiences of leadership. What influences women in their practice of leadership? How do they develop their leadership role and how do they maintain it?

In Chapter 2 we concentrated our focus on discussing what visual and metaphorical images can reveal to us about women's leadership as a social, cultural and political phenomenon. Our assumption in exploring the impact of photographs, pictures, metaphors and stereotypes is that the images they conjure up both shape, and are shaped by, social expectations of women leaders. Our discussion put forward the suggestion that what might initially seem to be fairly mundane day-to-day social interactions, such as referring to women as Queen Bees or Iron Maidens, have effects in terms of how women leaders come to be perceived. In analysing the implications of visual and metaphorical imagery of women leaders, the broader purpose of Chapter 2 was to reveal how such imagery maintains a tendency to focus on women leaders' individual styles and characteristics and excludes consideration of the sociocultural structures within which women live and work. This means we gain little insight into how social practices and processes impact upon women leaders, for example, the ways in which we make decisions or how we recruit leaders in organisations.

To contribute to the development of more in-depth understandings of women's leadership in this chapter, we explore in more detail how leading women negotiate and navigate their leadership 'route'. That is, how women become and sustain their role as leaders including the public and private resources they access for support. To us this suggested the need for a method of inquiry that encourages women leaders to reflect on, and make sense of, their experience as a first step in working towards a more contextual awareness of the nature and learning of leadership. This chapter therefore draws on in-depth interviews of two to three hours each with nine women leaders from a range of settings including politics, community activism, the not-for-profit sector, athletics, further education, self-employment and public service. The women leaders we interviewed are: Baroness May Blood, Northern Ireland community activist and life peer; Baroness Betty Boothroyd, former Speaker of the House of Commons, President of Fight for Sight, a UK charity dedicated to research into the prevention and treatment of blindness and eye disease; Judith Donovan, CBE, entrepreneur; Jackie Fisher, Chief Executive and Principal of Newcastle College; Dawn Gibbins, MBE, entrepreneur, founder and former Chairman of Flowcrete Group plc., a multinational manufacturing flooring business; Dame Tanni Grey Thompson, DBE, former Paralympian athlete, Vice Chair of the Women's Sports and Fitness Foundation and Chair of the Commission on the Future of Women's Sport; Baroness Rennie Fritchie, DBE, Civil Service Commissioner and; Rebecca Stephens, MBE, mountaineer and expedition leader. We interviewed one woman leader who wishes to remain anonymous and for whom we use the pseudonym Sayeeda Khan. She works at a senior level for a UK charitable organisation.

When interviewing the women we were concerned to let them narrate their experience of becoming leaders in as much detail as possible and so posed both general, as well as more focused and detailed questions. The more general questions were introduced to gain an understanding of the women's experiences from their perspective and so we, for example, asked them: 'How did you begin your career? How have you achieved your current role?'. More detailed questions asked the women to recall specific events and experiences that they believed were significant in the context of their public lives and leadership roles, for example: 'Can you think of any incidents when you've been at a low point and felt like throwing in the towel, and what has inspired you to keep going?'. The advantage of engaging with this relatively small number of interviewees is that it allows us to provide a voice for women who do not necessarily fit the leadership development patterns associated with modern/traditional organisational career structures. This is important because there is a gap of empirical research examining women's leadership outside business and corporate settings (Elliott and Stead, 2008).

Deciding to work with this select group of women was therefore a deliberate choice. As well as achieving the broader aim of extending the empirical base to contribute to critical understandings of leadership, we wanted the opportunity to gain insight into the experiences of women leaders operating within different contexts and roles. We wanted to develop an understanding of what influenced 'inspirational' leaders to achieve success in their careers, and of the ways in which they learned to be leaders. By interviewing women from different work contexts we hoped to gain more understanding in terms of whether being a woman makes a difference to their role as a leader and to their learning of leadership.

In addition to making sense of the sociocultural context of women's leadership learning, our intention in presenting their narratives is to highlight that women practise leadership in a variety of sectors. The majority of studies that examine women and leadership tend to draw on women who are working in business settings. These studies, for example, Cranfield School of Management's annual 'Female FTSE' report, have contributed a great deal in drawing attention to the low number of women in senior positions. In her introduction to the Female FTSE 2008 report (Sealy, Singh and Vinnicombe, 2008), Harriet Harman (Deputy Leader and Party Chair of the Labour Party, and Leader of the House of Commons) notes that the proportion of female directors in the UK's top companies has increased from 6.9 per cent in 1999 to 11.7 per cent in 2008. This indicates limited progress towards gender equality at boardroom level and she concludes that many British boardrooms are still 'no-go areas for women' (p. 3). She goes on to ask: 'What does it say to women in a company if all key decisions on the boardroom are taken by men?' (ibid.). This and related questions have preoccupied researchers who have variously focused on phenomena such as those discussed in the previous chapter (glass ceilings, glass cliffs) that illustrate the barriers women face in achieving leading positions in traditional organisational structures and how they are perceived and represented when they become leaders (Queen Bee, Iron Maiden, Selfless Heroine). As a consequence of both the type of settings where previous studies have taken place, as well as the small number of women in leadership positions, studies of women leaders outside the business context remain relatively rare. This then means our understanding of women's leadership is limited to women in business and therefore excludes experiences of leading women in other sectors. This chapter is therefore an opportunity to address this gap in empirical research and to present in some depth the ways in which leading women learn and experience leadership.

Women leaders' experiences

Researching into women's experiences of leadership revealed two important observations that lead to an understanding of women's leadership as dynamic and relational. By dynamic and relational we mean that the women's accounts can be interpreted as showing leadership operating on multiple levels and emerging from a series of relations in which women leaders play a central part: through their interactions with others, through the decisions they make, through activities they are involved with and in the way that leadership might be attributed to them. The first of the two observations that encourage us to take a dynamic and relational view is that women leaders draw upon multiple sources of experience both past and present in their practice of leadership including experiences in relation to paid and unpaid work, home, childhood and family life. A second observation is that women leaders' accounts do not draw upon their breadth of experience in a linear way. Rather their accounts tend to the non-linear moving easily between different areas of experience. Our research demonstrates these findings by indicating three particularly significant interconnected spheres of influence in the lives of women leaders that we will draw out in this chapter: relationship to others, relationship to place and relationship to work.

We have chosen to conceive of these spheres of influence as a Leadership Web (see Figure 3.1) in that they connect the leaders to their social and cultural setting and to their aspirations.

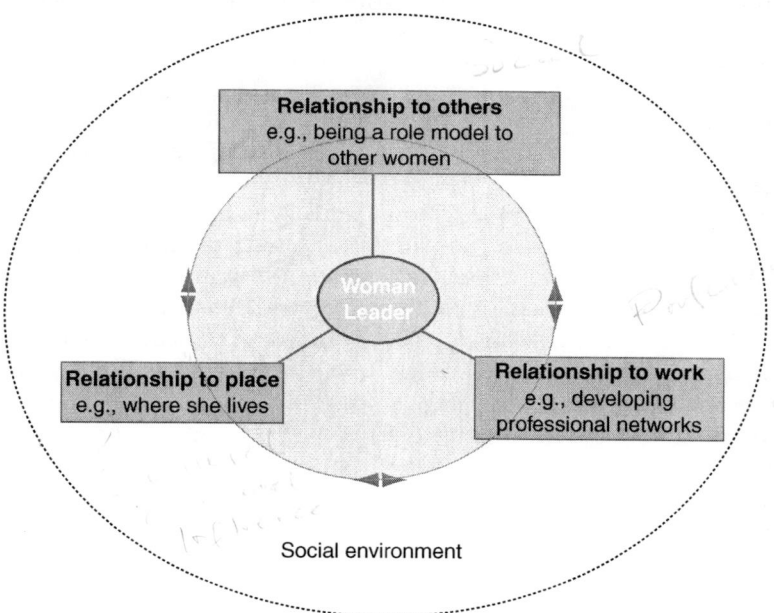

Figure 3.1 The Leadership Web: A model that shows how women's leadership is influenced by a range of interconnecting and dynamic relationships.

As a dynamic construction of leadership the spheres of influence that we identify are often overlapping and interwoven. For instance, relationships to others are often bound within the workplace and therefore part of a relationship to work. Equally, the leaders' relationship to place will be shaped by relationships to others as well as to the workplace. Therefore, while for clarity we describe the Leadership Web within the categories of the three spheres of influence, these descriptions necessarily overlap – they are not mutually exclusive – and in that regard they reflect the looping back and forth to different connections that our interviewees articulated.

Spheres of influence

Relationship to others

A common theme across all the interviews was the women leaders' relationship to other people. Our respondents' accounts emphasised their relationship as a woman to others including family relationships such as being a daughter or being a mother, and drawing on these unique female experiences in their leadership. The women leaders' accounts of their experience also highlighted either the presence or absence of role models and mentors, and the importance of developing networks and alliances including all female networks.

Many women leaders' accounts point to their family as being a source of inspiration and support. They also indicate how families nurture their determination to do better and enable them to move on. The experiences of Sayeeda Khan (senior leader in a UK charitable organisation) and Dame Tanni Grey Thompson (former Paralympian athlete) highlight this well. Sayeeda Khan found inspiration for her career choice from participating in armchair politics with her father. It was he, she asserts, who stimulated and encouraged her love of the law as a profession and her passion for human rights. She recalls a debate with him about the Yorkshire Ripper murders in the 1970s and early 1980s and discussing the case for the death penalty:

> My father and I often had very heated debates and I often – you know what it is like when you are a teenager – you know everything better and your father is a bit of a buffoon. But on this occasion my father turned round – and my father could be really, sometimes

quite arrogant in the way that he would put his argument across. But on this occasion he spoke very quietly and very calmly and not very emotionally and he said 'No the death penalty is wrong'. *(If you)* remember in the 1980s the death penalty wasn't as far beyond contemplation as it is now. In the Tory (*UK conservative*) party there were very real lively debates. Douglas Hurd (*former Home secretary*) at one point – got booed at Tory (*conservative*) Party conference as the home secretary for not supporting the death penalty. It was much closer to our experience and our reflections and our contemplations than it is now. And my father said to me 'the death penalty is absolutely wrong' and I said 'okay why?' And he said 'there is no justice in the world that will ever be 100% fool proof – no system in the world. But imagine you are the one innocent in a million that has been wrongly convicted and you are walking down that corridor for the last time and you are about to be killed. And you are saying to yourself or to God or to whoever you are speaking to 'I know that I didn't do this and they are about to kill me'. And it was incredibly powerful and that is why it has sort of stuck with me. Now of course there are many other very important and philosophical arguments against the death penalty. I wouldn't support the death penalty even if you could – which you never could – be 100% sure that – there are always other arguments about the value of human life and the dignity of individuals but that really, really stuck with me.

This relationship with her father, the ability to discuss and debate the law has been a cornerstone in her career. In her role today she continues to turn to her family for what she calls critical support; that is, having a group of people around her who can be honest and critical in the knowledge that they have her best interests at heart.

Dawn Gibbins is an entrepreneur and former Chairman of Flowcrete plc., a specialist flooring company founded in 1982 by Dawn and her father. Flowcrete is the UK market leader in specialist flooring with offices in 26 countries and manufacturing sites in eight countries. For Dawn, her family has been instrumental in developing, supporting and encouraging her throughout her career. Her business success today began during a kitchen table discussion about an idea from her mother over 25 years ago. As a designer of flooring, Dawn's father had worked for many major companies but had never put a commercial price tag on his inventions. Having designed a sugar resistant floor for Mars in 1982, her father was about to sell the formulation to them for £2000, when her mother suggested that he and Dawn begin their own business. As a result Dawn describes herself as a homegrown leader:

> So we set up together in 1982 when I was 23 and I became a Managing Director at the age of 23, setting up this business. And really my career has been developing this company. So I'm really a home-grown leader, home-grown Managing Director and Chair.

Tanni Grey Thompson also cites her family as a continuing supportive and critical presence. Her parents and husband, she says, have been instrumental in helping her achieve her athletic success:

> And I think sometimes because I am strong willed I don't think it is very positive but I think sometimes it can cloud some of the decisions I make because I can be a bit impulsive without making decisions and that is where my parents – my Dad is still alive – but they were great because my Dad is very measured, very considered – he is an architect you know very organised, you know 'you don't just do that you think ten steps ahead and work your way back' whereas I am just like 'oh I am going to do that'. And that was very useful when I was growing up because he would say 'well what about' 'do that a bit differently'. And Ian, my husband, is quite like that as well because he is an industrial scientist so he is very kind of ordered and thinks about consequences. So they have always been a bit of a calming influence on me I think. They make me think about stuff so I think it has always just been there.

Interviewees then emphasise the significance of family relationships in being critical and supportive. While the family acts as a support, we did however observe that the early years of a woman's life, their experience of being female and the significance of female influences in shaping their future figure particularly prominently in women leaders' experiences. The women leaders spoke of how they drew especially on female role models and female experiences from their childhood. Their upbringing and experience of young adulthood in the local community and in the workplace also emerged as noteworthy. These experiences exert important influence both in the development of the woman to her leadership role today and in her continuing development.

Tanni Grey Thompson (former Paralympian athlete) and Baroness May Blood, (community activist and life peer) talk about the importance of their mothers. As May Blood observes:

People very often ask me who would have been my role models. I suppose my only role model in my life would have been my mother. And my mother was a very gentle woman but there was a determination about my mother that – when you said something you knew she meant it.

She talks of the significance of her mother in shaping her ambition. In her early years she says:

my mother was a cook and all the years that I can remember my mother worked out[side the home] and I went to a little school and I passed the dreaded 11 plus – what we call it back in Northern Ireland – my father wanted me to go and learn a language because he said the future of the world was in language. I wanted to be a schoolteacher. I hated school but I thought the teacher had the power of … mother.

Tanni Grey Thompson acknowledges her mother as hugely influential in encouraging her self belief, 'just because of the way she dealt with stuff. … My Mum used to say to me "don't moan about it – do something". My Mum's influence is still there'.

Being a mother also provides inspiration for women leaders. Sayeeda Khan talks about motherhood as a powerful resource for her in her work:

I am a mother, which to me is a pretty awesome grown up thing. I am sure it is the same whether you are fifteen or thirty-five but it is this – it both connects you to the rest of humanity in a way that you never anticipated. From the moment you walk down the street pregnant and you see another pregnant woman – they might be very posh or they might be from a council estate but there is a basic human connection. Or when you are pushing the pram – so you have got that connection with the human race and also a sense of not being a child anymore.

Being a mother, she asserts, helps her understand what it is like to be vulnerable and dependant. She likens facing difficult decisions in her work, particularly in relation to the treatment of others, to the responsibility of caring for a young child:

whenever you have insecurities you can't afford to indulge them because you're responsibly the child's mother and that is your privilege and your awesome responsibility.

The relationship of being a mother or being a daughter can be seen to hold particular importance given a scarcity of female role models. Women leaders' accounts illustrate that the way in which they relate to others is also impacted upon by the presence or absence of female role models. Having role models of pioneering women is important for many in that it shows that leadership is possible for women.

Jackie Fisher, Principal and Chief Executive of Newcastle College in the UK, believes that being exposed to other senior women can help women leaders find ways in which they want to lead:

there's something about observing other women who are perceived to be effective leaders, looking at how they behave and conduct themselves and think is there anything to learn from that

A further example is provided by Sayeeda Khan who felt she was fortunate to have the first woman treasury solicitor as her mentor and role model during her time as a lawyer at the Home Office: 'as a young woman I felt positively supported and inspired'. Being able to observe and learn from this other woman first-hand helped Sayeeda Khan to see that not only could women achieve as leaders but that they could achieve brilliantly.

Conversely, the absence of role models is also significant for women. As many women leaders are pioneers they therefore have little or no access to other senior women. The lack of predecessors and therefore existent role models has been liberating in some ways for women. For example, Baroness Betty Boothroyd, first female Speaker in the House of Commons, <u>found that having no predecessor</u> <u>enabled her to make a break with tradition and to do things</u> her own <u>way</u> including not wearing the traditional wig:

> I have done everything my way. I don't have role models. ... I hope I am not an imitation of anybody ... there was nobody I wanted to copy. I decided I wasn't going to wear the wig you know. I had my own style.

For Tanni Grey Thompson, becoming a Paralympian team leader and an athlete with a disability were not roles that were readily visible when she was growing up. Therefore, she had no one specifically to relate to or to emulate, or conversely, no role model to set limitations. She says:

> I have never wanted to be somebody or be like somebody. I have always just wanted – oh God it sounds awful doesn't it? – To be me. But I think as well when I was growing up, I started using the chair when I was seven, you didn't see disabled people. So I probably – if I had seen someone who was a wheelchair user doing something I might have related to it more. Whereas I didn't relate to non-disabled sports people in the same way. And it was always just a bit sort of – I don't know – there just wasn't one person that I grew up sort of looking at. My experience of disability growing up was you had Sammy Richardson on Crossroads who wasn't really disabled cos he could walk you know and you didn't see him in his chair very often. And that was it – you didn't see disabled people. You didn't see disabled people out on the streets let alone on TV programmes or in the media or – if you look at recent history people like Roosevelt – they hid the fact that he was a wheelchair user. So there weren't disabled people in the way that there are now.

Similar to Betty Boothroyd's lack of role models this was to some extent liberatory for Tanni. Not having any particular social expectation made her feel that she could do what she wanted to do.

While women leaders may not have easy access to other senior women because of the pioneering nature of their position, they talk about the encouragement of other women or role modeling as part of their role. Betty Boothroyd for example, made it her task to be available to support new women MPs. Of her time in the House of Commons, she says:

> Well when I was speaker I hope that I gave a lot of encouragement to women MPs who came in 1997. There were a great number of women MPs who came in then and I was always available to them and talked to them – just sort of sympathetically … when making their maiden speech – I used to sit at the end of my chair and there was a lot to do with body language and eye contact and willing them on and being helpful in that way.

May Blood too sees her role in the House of Lords as an opportunity to encourage other women:

> being the first woman here I have got to make a success of it in the hope that some women from Northern Ireland will follow me.

With fewer role models available to women leaders, the development of social networks and alliances play an important role for women leaders. Typically, these are very diverse and due to a lack of other senior women not just confined to the workplace. Many women leaders have enduring personal networks that they rely on as critical friends including family and friends who are not necessarily work related but are personally supportive.

The women's experiences illuminate that drawing on support from other women is important because women are treated differently. While the networks they draw on aren't necessarily all female, women's networks do play a vital role in helping women leaders deal with the isolation of being a woman in their position. Baroness Rennie Fritchie, Civil Service Commissioner, for example, talks about the support, motivation and encouragement gained from having a woman's network:

> My women's network … we all had really tough times at different times and publicly tough times. We were all women leaders and all hit the headlines not for what (we) did but often for standing up for something.

In summary, we can observe that the relationships that women leaders have with others are notably framed by the women's gender. Access to role models, or being a role model, is important for women leaders as it both showcases women's leadership and illustrates its credibility. Conversely, a lack of role models is seen from these accounts to be used as a way to create difference and to develop ambition. Exploring women's relationships with others highlights that women leaders gain inspiration from a range of sources beyond the workplace, drawing on personal networks of families and friends to sustain them throughout their career. They also look to their relationships as a woman such as being a daughter or a mother, and to their relationships with other women such as being part of a women's network to support and sustain them in their practice.

Relationship to place

Women's leadership practice is also shaped by their relationship to place. We refer to place as the physical and geographical location in which the women leaders were brought up and in which they live. However tied to the physical and geographical place is a historical context and social, political and cultural values. Therefore in relationship to place we also observe that women's accounts of their experiences provide a picture of a particular social, political, historical and cultural landscape. We begin by exploring the connection that the women have to particular locations and how this then has implications for a woman's social standing, their 'place' in society.

Baroness Betty Boothroyd, first woman Speaker of the House of Commons, attributes her success in part to her northern background;

> I was just going to succeed. I felt that all the time. You could just say it was determination and I don't know what else – grit, north country attitude.

Betty Boothroyd's awareness of her upbringing as a young woman and the opportunities and limitations afforded by her particular community fuelled a determination to progress.

For Judith Donovan, entrepreneur, women's lesser social status was particularly connected to her socio-geographical location. In her view, being a woman who wanted to achieve was particularly challenging when she began her business in 1982:

[T]hen we were much more of an endangered species, particularly in the North, particularly in Yorkshire and very particularly in Bradford where I think women managers were like rocking horse shit. And those challenges are, firstly about actually registering on the radar. ... It wasn't that people looked at you, it's not the Doctor Johnson thing you know, four legs or two legs but remarkable she does it. People just didn't even see that you were there because the concept of an ambitious woman or a woman who was successful against a man's template of success, which is non-existent. So it's not about pushing through the glass ceiling, it's actually about having sort of nose up against a sweet shop window and banging on the door and saying, 'I am outside, will you let me in?'

She provides a further example of when she joined a catalogue company and was acknowledged to be a great worker. It was nonetheless made clear to her that there was a limit to what she might achieve as a woman in that particular location:

(*the company*) were saying to me, "You can be our advertising manager for the rest of your life Judith, because you are doing a wonderful job, but you can forget any chance of getting into general management to climb the ladder, because that doesn't happen in Bradford." It didn't because Bradford had a mill mentality.

May Blood sees her aspirations and achievements as integral to her locality and work community. During her early career her observation that women and children were accorded lesser status became instrumental in her ambition to bring about change. Her belief that women and children have equal rights in society has been shaped by growing up in Northern Irish society that saw, she says, 'women and children as a throwaway'. She describes the mill where she worked from the age of 14:

Very poor conditions. Wages practically non-existent. I mean some of the early memories I have of the mill – women working with water lapping round their ankles, women running in and out to breast feed children and coming back and all that kind of thing and domestic violence was a big thing you know.

This harsh environment where she was exposed to issues of poverty, poor education and gender inequality was for her a microcosm of Northern Ireland society: 'you are', she says, 'a product of what you live through'. These experiences, being part of this particular mill community, helped her she asserts, understand her own position as a woman in society and the position of others. Her work as a community activist provides an example of the social positioning of women as having fewer rights. As a part of her work in Belfast during the so-called 'troubles' in Northern Ireland, she was engaged in a project that sought to bring Protestant and Roman Catholic communities together. Moving between the two communities was considered highly dangerous work during that period and involved crossing what was known as the peace line. This was a wall standing over 23 feet high, erected in west and north Belfast, to separate Protestant and Roman Catholic communities. Ironically, she realised that had she been a man it would have been very difficult to cross the peace line as this would have been quickly noticed and seen as threatening. However, she found that as a woman she and her work weren't taken seriously and these perceptions enabled her to cross back and forth as she needed to:

> I was only a woman. ... What would a woman know about constitutional things? So let them get on with the community things and in those days community was all about women.

While her perceived lesser social status afforded her the advantage of being able to cross the peace line, it also positioned her and her work as being of little importance.

Jackie Fisher, recognises too that women are positioned differently and links this to geographical place. She observes the dominance of a culture in leadership approaches and forums in the north east of England 'which is not about women'. She says:

> I think there are still a number of individuals who are, what I would call, unreconstructed, in terms of where they come from, in terms of gender. And that probably is not challenged enough. Do these cause me a problem in my day-to-day life as a leader, no not really, because you just get on with it. But I think if you get two or three women together, particularly women who are new to the north east, they

will comment on how different it is culturally here to be a leader, than it is [in] other regions.

The women leaders' relationship to place is then marked not only by the particular geographical location but also by the way in which the social and cultural values of that location view a woman's place in that particular society. The women leaders' accounts might therefore be interpreted as examples of how women are constructed and positioned within the particular social community to which the women belong. May Blood in an account of her years working in a linen mill in Northern Ireland observes that a woman's place in the mill was viewed as subordinate to men. She recalls:

> The one and only strike we had I remember my employer telling me he had given me a job 'what more did I want'.

In spite of the mill workforce being predominantly women she says:

> out of 450 people who worked in the mill there would have been about 90 men but they were all in strategic positions ... as a woman my expectations were too low.

With the linen mill employing women mainly from working class backgrounds, a woman's place here might be seen as shaped by class and gender.

Such experiences appear to serve to fuel a determination that opportunities will be different for girls in the future. May Blood, for example, has been determined since her years in the mill to fight for educational opportunities for children and to champion women's and children's rights. While some of the experiences the women refer to may stem from the 1950s and 1960s, women leaders are quick to point out that women's relationship to place is still determined by being female. Rennie Fritchie, for instance, talks about the connection between political legislation and a woman's place in society. She contends that while discrimination may not always be so blatant it is nonetheless still there. She says:

> there is something about not thinking people like me are historical and of a time when life was tough for women ... underneath the icing and the marzipan it is still the same.

In this quote she asserts that in spite of legislation such as the Equal Opportunities Act (the icing and the marzipan), women still face particular difficulties. A woman's place, it might be interpreted, is different from a man's and has lesser status. This status we might argue then becomes manifest in expectations of what girls and women might or might not achieve.

Jackie Fisher, in her role as Chief Executive and Principal of one of the UK's largest colleges of further education, finds that her experience of working with young women is different to that of young men in that they have lesser expectations beyond college. She observes:

> there's a lot of gender issues around how women see themselves, see their ability to contribute and have some time horizon beyond school.

Sayeeda Khan also observed from her schooldays a lack of expectation of girls, and in particular girls with less affluent backgrounds:

> [T]here was no great natural differential in our potential and our ability but the expectations.

Race as well as class makes a difference. For instance, Sayeeda Khan felt that, as the daughter of Asian immigrant parents, there were expectations that she would achieve professional status:

> [O]ne of the things you get from your sort of lower/middle class Asian parents who have both been to university is that you could theoretically do whatever you wanted to do. And there is no question that you could of course go to university.

Women's stories demonstrate that relationship to place is complex. Their accounts reveal connections to particular physical locations, such as a linen mill or particular geographical places such as being from the North. They also talk about their place as a woman in society, their relationship as a woman to the society to which they belong both at a micro level, whether that is at a school or a workplace and at a macro level, to a larger community, for example, through being working class or Asian. Their relationship to place, whether it be geographical or social, is shaped by their gender, by their being female. As women they see themselves occupying places that are different to men including places of lesser social standing and of different expectations. This might be described as women being positioned in particular ways because they are women.

For many of the women leaders whose experiences are described here, this positioning while raising barriers also acts as a stimulus for their determination and ambition. Relationship to place then can play the additional role of bringing into relief for these women those issues that are significant for them and their community such as women's and children's rights. Relationship to place therefore remains a cornerstone to their ongoing leadership practice.

Sphere of influence: Women's relationship to work

The women leaders' accounts showed the significance of their relationship to work and, in particular, their accounts demonstrated how this relationship had been influenced by early work experiences and the location of that work. For example, May Blood's accounts of working in a linen mill as we relate in the relationship to place section above. What emerges as particularly significant, complex and often problematic for women leaders however is how women are positioned as workers and employees. Women's relationship to work is in many cases defined by the barriers they encounter. The women's accounts reveal however that their relationship to work is also defined by how they maneouvre and negotiate their leadership in the face of barriers including their development of professional networks and alliances.

In discussing their working lives women leaders observe the difference of being a woman in a managerial or senior role. Judith Donovan, for example, remembers that women were actively discouraged from seeking managerial roles and were expected to make way for men. She recalls as a young woman in the 1970s:

> [After] joining [a large automotive manufacturing company] as a graduate trainee in marketing and being told that they've got too many people wanting to do marketing so would the women go off and do personnel instead. And this was before the Equal Opportunities Act was passed, big companies could do stuff like that. You know, and having to fight that at 21 years old, fresh out of university, your first job, this exciting job, you are looking

forward to it and then someone is trying to sort of put you back in the box.

May Blood began her working life in a linen mill in Belfast at the age of 14 and remained an employee until the mill's closure some 38 years later. Her early experiences of working in the mill highlighted for her that women's relationship to work was viewed and rewarded differently to that of men and that this offered her a platform for challenge. Her story of working as a trade union representative highlights workplace expectations of women and also what women's expectations are of the workplace:

> I remember being in a room full of men and they were arguing about the World Cup and that their firm would not allow them to watch the match live. The day before I went to that I was asking my employer for toilet rolls. And that taught me that women were not asking for nearly enough. We were just taking whatever was given. The one and only strike we had I remember my employer telling me that he had given me a job 'what more did I want?' It was that whole attitude – the mill was predominantly women – that was the whole attitude to (work) ... pin money. The whole attitude was that 'we don't need to pay any attention to them'. Even in the room I worked in the two men pushed a truck but they had far more wages than anybody (the women) who was making and delivering the most beautiful production of stuff: table linen, bed linen for all the big companies. ... And so I began to use the union more or less as a platform.

Betty Boothroyd observes that in UK society it is women who continue to be faced with the responsibilities of family life and the dilemma of choosing between family and career. Her relationship with work highlights for her the complexity of balancing work and home life and that the choices and responsibilities in how work and home are managed typically are seen as women's domain:

> I think it is extremely difficult for women who marry and have children. I admire and respect them – who can go into a career and have all of that as well. I doubt that I could have done it. I am not sure that I could have done it. I don't think that I could divide

myself up to have a domestic life ... for women to do a big public life and to do that at the same time is extremely difficult. And I always say that you either have to have – I have always said it even when I was in the Commons – you either have to have the gem of a granny or enough money for a nanny. That is what you have got to have. And particularly for women in Parliament who have to leave them in the country somewhere and spend their week in London. And a lot of the young women here – if you have interviewed them you will probably find that their husbands have become househusbands ... you know you have to make a decision. You can't have everything in life. You really can't. You have to give some things up. Now if you want to give your career up – that is entirely up to you. But if you want a career and manage your home and family at the same time then you have to provide for that home.

Betty Boothroyd expands further on the gendered nature of work in her observation of the lesser status accorded to women's work and achievements in relation to her determination to develop a memorial (since unveiled in 2007) to recognise women's role in the Second World War:

we are the only nation that hasn't got a monument to those women: Australia, Canada, New Zealand, America – they have all got their monuments to pay tribute to their women and nothing in this country.

This lack of acknowledgement for women at work is also noted by Rennie Fritchie. Talking about her career in management she recalls:

[W]e *(women)* had such evident discrimination against us, such blatant behaviour.

Indeed the women leaders all talked about barriers they have encountered in entering the workplace and at work. In some cases, they observed, these barriers are not always concrete, visible barriers but barriers of perception that become the accepted norm.

For instance, Sayeeda Khan observes that women seem to have to work harder to get ahead and are subject to fewer opportunities. Her account of leaving pupilage in chambers illustrates this well when she recalls that men were more likely than women to get offered prestigious positions, even compared to those women who had first class degrees from Oxford.

Tanni Grey Thompson found that becoming a mother brought with it a perception that she would have less commitment to her sport. May Blood found that decision-making roles in political parties were not readily available to women because they were not perceived as having anything to contribute. Dawn Gibbins found that in the male-dominated industry of manufacturing women are scarce and often don't have access to the social circles, such as the golf club or meetings in the bar, where important decisions are often made.

What continues to motivate these women and sustain their focus is, they say, their determination. Rebecca Stephens, mountaineer and expedition leader, believes that focus is 'the first quality of leadership', and that in her field the authenticity that focus brings to a leader is what inspires others to contribute. The women interviewed in our study felt that clarity of focus is instrumental in enabling them to find ways to negotiate and manoeuvre in the face of barriers they encounter as women.

May Blood relates how she established a political party, the Coalition Party, in 1996. In 1994, at the time leading up to the peace talks in Northern Ireland she enquired of the minister for Northern Ireland whether women would be present at the peace talks and the response was they would be if they were elected. She says:

> we didn't need another political party – God knows we have enough of them in Northern Ireland. But women were never going to be at the front table.

May Blood used this opportunity to negotiate a leadership role. With a group of other women she went on to set up the Northern Ireland Women's Coalition Party and as a result the party did get two seats at the peace talks' table.

Judith Donovan provides a further example of negotiating a leadership role. She was keen to do something for the community but as a woman she found that she didn't have access to the clubs and societies that had connections and enabled such contributions. Instead, she found herself sitting on a government steering group that no one was interested in. It was this experience that gave her a route into working with Quangos (quasi non-governmental organisations) which have helped her develop her career as a public leader. Here she describes how this came about:

> Now it all started undoubtedly with the Trading Enterprise Council in Bradford and that was because I was making a nuisance of myself in Bradford saying I want to do something for the community, I want to contribute my leadership skills, I want to do more than just be an employer but as a woman I was being told to sod off because the mechanisms for things like Rotaries and Round Tables and Lions, that women couldn't even join, and everyone was saying to me the only thing you can do is become a politician and stand to go on the council, if you want to put something back into Bradford. And I was saying, I'm not kissing papers, I'm not pratting around with that sort of local democratic stuff because I'm trying to offer my skill set, which is an entrepreneur business skill set. ... So then somebody said, the Government is in town, they are forming a steering group, they want to set up this quango thing that nobody has ever heard of, come along to the meeting. And I went along to the meeting and realised that nobody was terribly excited about it, nobody understood it, nobody was terribly bothered and I thought aha, and I said, "Well should I have a look at it?" And as a result of that I developed this strategic plan and as a result of that the Government invited me to chair it, which suited them because there was only one female chairman and that was me and I was the youngest chairman in the country.

These examples illustrate that women leaders, while faced with barriers at work, nonetheless find ways in which to navigate such barriers and develop their leadership.

The women leaders' accounts illustrate the importance of developing professional networks and alliances as a significant way to deal with barriers and to develop their leadership. When discussing women leaders' relationship to others we highlighted the importance of family relationships and personal networks. In addition to those networks the women described shifting and dynamic professional networks and alliances. Professional networks and alliances have significance for all of the women in that they support their work and are important in retaining focus and ambition.

Professional networks and alliances among the women interviewees tended to be multi-layered and more fluid than personal networks, with different networks and alliances taking on varying importance at different times. Professional networks are characterised by their multi-layered nature and diversity. Rebecca Stephens talks about a range of overlapping networks that she is part of in each expedition including for example, a team of mountaineers, a Sherpa team, a logistics team, a back-up support team, press and media team, funding and sponsorship team and individuals whom she might turn to for advice. This multi-layered, broad and complex network may have similar elements for each mountaineering expedition but may not include the same individuals with the same aspirations and will take on different emphases throughout an expedition. For instance, at the early stages of an expedition planning, logistics and funding parts of the network may take prominence, during the actual expedition the climbing teams will be central and at different points along the way the press and media will be of core importance. This kind of network then may resemble a moving three-dimensional map where different parts of the network come into relief at different stages. Each expedition may then be seen to have such a network map with networks and alliances being reconstituted and reconfigured for different projects.

In this way networks and alliances can be seen as constantly evolving and developing in order to reflect the women's position and context at any one time. Sayeeda Khan cites her professional networks and alliances as important for her in having the courage to stick to her principles and in being 'prepared to stick your neck out' for what you believe in.

Rebecca Stephens also finds that her networks and alliances have special significance during difficult times. In her book, she writes:

> [W]hen you take a leap of faith, and walk a path, aligned to your desires, other people recognize your authenticity and want to help. No longer battling with yourself, you are no longer battling with the world – and everything flows with considerably less resistance.
>
> (Heller and Stephens 2005: 53)

These accounts accord with research that shows that role models and sponsorship are important in advancing leaders' careers (Perriton, 2006). Women have fewer female role models, sponsors, mentors and support networks in the workplace. The accounts of Betty Boothroyd and May Blood for example, in our exploration of relationship to others, highlight the lack of role models and professional alliances for women, and they believe it is important for them to encourage other women. Perhaps as a result of limited access to networks and role models, our women leaders talked about drawing on wider and more diverse networks beyond the workplace as well as making alliances within the work environment. For example, Sayeeda Khan talks about drawing on networks that encompass colleagues from a range of other workplaces. Rennie Fritchie belongs to a network of women leaders for support.

Women leaders' relationship to work then emerges as a relationship which is defined by the positioning of women in the workplace. The women leaders' accounts show that as women they encounter barriers including barriers of perception and of expectation. These barriers, while blocking and excluding, also appear to act as stimuli for the women leaders to negotiate and develop leadership. The women's relationship to work is also marked by fluid and multiple networks and alliances that they claim enable them to maintain focus and determination.

Conclusion

In this chapter we have described accounts from nine women leaders to identify three main broad spheres of influence, pictured in Figure 3.1, in women's leadership roles and practice. We have labelled these in terms of relationships: relationship to others, relationship to place and relationship to work. The women's accounts show that these relationships are not static but dynamic, shifting and often overlapping. The personal and professional networks and alliances they draw upon for example, span their relationships to others, to place and to work and shift to accommodate their current role and development.

We also observe that within these spheres of influence there are multiple relationships which operate at multiple levels. For instance, in the sphere we label relationship to work, the women develop and access multiple networks including personal networks, professional networks, networks that include people from diverse organisations and women-only networks. Our sphere of relationship to place provides an example of relationships operating at multiple levels, such as a woman leader's relationship to her immediate workplace and her relationship to society more broadly. The sphere, relationship to others, offers yet a different aspect of relationality, for example, the way in which the women leaders interact with others such as accessing other women for support or acting as role models for aspiring leaders. The women leaders' accounts, we claim, show that the nature of such relationships is inflected by gender, class and race. We thus begin to see how leadership might be understood as relational in different ways and from different perspectives. For example, we can conceptualise leadership as relational at a micro level such as through interactions with others and at macro levels such as through relationships to the wider social environment. Furthermore we can also observe how relationality might be explored further through a range of lenses, such as gender, race or class.

In the following chapter we aim to develop our understanding of leadership as relational further through a gender lens. Our discussion of data has led us to highlight how the women's accounts of their leadership practice are shaped by their gender. For example, in the relationship to the workplace the accounts show that women have to deal with particular barriers that can exclude and isolate them. These accounts then lead us to question, to what extent does gender impact upon women's leadership? How does gender matter?

4
Gender Matters

> I think certainly in the Northeast, maybe less so in
> the rest of the North of England, I don't really know,
> there are fewer woman leaders than you might find
> in other parts of the country and therefore there is
> not a kind of a natural peer group to work within.
> It is not unusual to find yourself as the only one to
> maybe, on a good day, one of three women, with
> significant numbers of men in a meeting or at an
> event. And that in itself poses challenges because
> there's definitely a dominant culture in leadership
> and forums in the Northeast, which is not about
> women.
>
> —Jackie Fisher, Principal and Chief Executive of
> Newcastle College

Here Jackie Fisher describes being in the minority as a woman leader.
She goes on to say that this can bring with it challenges. In this
chapter we want to discuss the extent to which gender matters in
women's leadership. Does it matter if you are female and how does
it matter? The women's accounts described in Chapter 3 led us to
observe that much of their experience is shaped by being female in
terms of social perceptions of them and of how women are positioned
in the workplace. This then raises questions around the extent to
which gender is significant in the practice of women's leadership.

We begin the chapter by discussing conceptions of gender and
presenting an understanding of gender that takes a relational perspective and operates at multiple levels. We then exemplify the
significance of gender in women's leadership experience and explore
its impact through the use of Amy Wharton's analytical framework

of gender (2005). We do this by drawing on data from our own study of women's leadership and by referring to other studies of women's leadership including work by Coleman (2005a, 2005b), Eagly and Carli (2007), Hartman (1999), Levinson (1996) and Vinnicombe and Bank (2003). Drawing on a range of studies from the past decade offers breadth and depth to our analysis and enables us to broaden our research from a mainly UK focus to draw on a greater range of sectors. Therefore work by Coleman (2005a, 2005b) and Vinnicombe and Bank (2003) for example, target a specific grouping – UK school head teachers and Veuve Cliquot award winners respectively– and are particularly concerned with leadership. Levinson's (1996) study works across a range of US women from different backgrounds and professions with a view of exploring more widely the experiences that women have at different stages of their lives. Eagly and Carli's work (2007) draws widely on contemporary, and mainly US examples, in order to explore the obstacles women encounter in becoming leaders and how they might overcome them. Hartman's study (1999) is a collection of conversations with what she calls 'powerful women' in the US who don't always fit easily into a conventional understanding of leadership. For instance, she includes interviews with a journalist and novelist as well as a social scientist and feminist activist. These women are leaders, she argues, in a broader and more developed understanding of the term that has more currency in developing countries than industrialised nations. This understanding embraces women who have the ability to influence and mobilise in a range of settings, such as neighbourhood communities and regional sites, as well as through a variety of media including teaching, writing or by being actively engaged in local projects (Hartman, 1999: 3).

By drawing on these studies in addition to our own we aim to offer an appreciation of how gender impacts upon women's leadership practice. The chapter concludes by identifying how women leaders are positioned by gendered practices. It then considers what the implications of the impact of gender might be for women's leadership identity and for women's leadership development.

Understanding gender

Gender is acknowledged to be a highly contested term that may be interpreted in multiple ways (Acker, 1992; Gatrell and Swan, 2008).

Ashcraft and Mumby (2004), in their examination of gender and feminist scholarly work in critical approaches to organisation studies, provide a useful overview of how gender has been conceptualised in organisational research. They note that over the past three decades gender has largely been presented as an aspect of organisational life that, while having relevance to different organisational issues such as leadership, is nonetheless viewed as a factor to be considered, rather than as integral to understandings of how organisations operate.

One reason for this blind spot might be the result of organisations generally being considered 'gender neutral'. Eagly and Carli (2007) explain gender neutral organisations as workplaces that present themselves as having no bias in favour of either sex. Acker (1995: 139) refers to gender neutrality in terms of what she calls 'the gendered logic of organization'. She describes this gendered logic as an assumption that the ideal worker is gender neutral, that is, that her/his performance remains unaffected by prevailing gender discourses and so can offer complete commitment to the organisation. This implicit model of the ideal worker who has minimal commitments and can therefore devote themselves entirely to the workplace – for instance, by working long hours and socialising after work – is typically someone who has no other obligations such as care of dependents or children. This model of the ideal worker thus favours the male, who even with domestic commitments is more likely to be able to delegate these to a spouse (Eagly and Carli, 2007) or other female family members. Conceptualising organisations as gender neutral is therefore problematic as the ideal worker is not gender neutral but is implicitly male.

Alvesson and Due Billing (1997) recognise other concerns that emerge from the failure to attend to gender. They observe that the lack of consideration given to gender in organisational studies and a masculine dominance in academic and organisational life shapes the research we conduct and the knowledge we produce. This then has the effect of reinforcing an implicit, taken-for-granted view that organisations are gender neutral and leads to masculinity being viewed as the managerial (Calas and Smircich, 1996; Lamsa and Sintonen, 2001) and leadership norm. Not only does this prevent us from recognising the legitimacy of female experiences in the workplace but also, as Acker (1998) contends, hinders us from exploring power relationships and everyday issues of gender subordination in organisations.

A further reason why the fundamental nature of gender might be ignored is to view gender from a 'biological' perspective. This perspective sees gender as natural and static leading to a binary categorisation of male and female, where our biology defines how we are different.

Gatrell and Swan (2008) however note a shift, by contemporary social theorists, from defining gender as natural, static and pre-existing to an understanding of gender as a social construction. That is, 'gender – and, in fact, other social categories, such as race, sexuality and disability – are seen as the result of human social processes, actions, language, thought and practices' (p. 4). Gender is not just about the organising of bodies they claim, 'but bifurcates the whole social world into segregated domains in the workplace, in cultural practices and in the home', (p. 4).

Viewing gender as a dynamic process, created and given meaning through social structures, processes and practices then encourages us to understand gender as what Ashcraft and Mumby term 'a basic pillar of organising' (2004: xiv).

Gender and women's leadership

Recognising that organising, managing and leading are not gender neutral activities but are rather shaped by fundamental organising practices such as gender is significant for our study of women's leadership for a number of reasons. Viewing gender as a 'basic pillar of organising' (Ashcraft and Mumby, 2004: xiv) enables us to examine more closely women leaders' accounts of the social practices and processes that constitute their leadership activity. In particular this perspective helps us to explore the assumptions and understandings that define such practices and processes, and to gain some insight into the power relationships and interests that they support (Acker, 1995). Understanding gender as a fundamental organising principle also enables us to challenge what Alvesson and Due Billing (1997: 2) refer to as the irrational 'ways of thinking and acting as well as social structures, that prevent almost half of the labour force from being fully utilized in terms of their qualifications and talents'. In other words, taking gender as an analytical lens helps us to uncover the barriers that women encounter in the workplace. Importantly, understanding gender as a social construction also has resonance with shifting ideas of leadership. As we have discussed in Chapter 1 leadership research is increasingly moving away from viewing leadership as an individual activity isolated from its social, cultural or political context. Rather, leadership research is shifting to an understanding of leadership practice and its development as dynamic, situated and socially constructed that is developed and shaped by social practices and structures including organisational cultures. This shift recognises the importance of context where attention is given for example, to the geographical places where individuals practise leadership and also of 'relationships of interdependence between leaders, the organization(s) and the context' (Morrell and Hartley, 2006: 494). Morrell and Hartley explain these interdependent relationships as leadership being relationally configured and this is in keeping with the findings from our accounts of women leaders in Chapter 3 and with previous work (Elliott and Stead, 2008). We identify how the women's experiences are seen to be given shape and meaning by dynamic and shifting relationships that lead us to view leadership as a social network of practice. Understanding leadership in this way then calls for an exploration of the fundamental, social and organisational practices such as gender, race and class that produce and reproduce such networks of practice (Broadbridge and Hearn, 2008). We acknowledge that such organisational practices interrelate and as Wharton (2005) says, shape people's experiences of the world, for example, a white middle-class female leader will have different experiences to a black working-class leader. Our examination of the accounts of women leaders illustrates this, for example, the account from May Blood of her working-class background in Chapter 3. However, as we outline in our introduction, our primary focus in this book is on gender.

Conceptualising gender as fundamental to organising, managing and leading, therefore enables us to view gender as operating at multiple levels, through relationships, through social practices, processes, activities and interactions (Acker, 1995; Wharton, 2005). This complex, dynamic view of gender then encourages us to take a critical stance to not only the social practices and processes of leading but also to the knowledge they produce, for example, how particular views or power relations are privileged and remain dominant (Swan et al., 2009). With a focus on the accounts of women leaders' interactions and the processes and activities that shape their experiences, we are therefore in a position to expand our knowledge of what constitutes leadership, and most particularly to examine what constitutes women's leadership.

Gender operating at multiple levels

In this next section we take forward the conceptualisation of gender as dynamic and operating at multiple levels. We explore in particular the impact of gender on women's leadership practice and their learning of leadership by employing what Amy Wharton (2005) identifies as contextual approaches.

In her discussion of gender she notes a shift from theoretical approaches that view gender as operating at an individual level, for example, gender residing in personalities, characteristics and attributes, to gender as relational and rooted in social interactions, practices and processes. This shift is significant in that it recognises agency and change. As Volman and ten Dam (1998: 532) put it:

> What is considered feminine and masculine is a historical and cultural product, a 'social construction', and is subject to change and internal contradictions. The socially constructed categories of femininity and masculinity interact in complex ways with other categories, such as ethnicity, class and age.

Thus, taking this perspective for women leaders, gender is not a given, but rather is actively constructed and reconstructed through their daily leadership activities.

In contrast the notion of gender operating at an individual level and residing in personalities and characteristics can place men and women in particular rigid conceptions of leadership. Indeed Hartman (1999: 10) in her edited collection of conversations with women leaders notes that 'early studies of female traits were merely feeding back preconceived views about women's lack of leadership ability'.

This has resonance with our discussion in Chapter 2 where we study stereotypes of women including particular images of Margaret Thatcher that emerged in the 1980s depicting her as an Iron Lady. This stereotypic portrayal, we suggested, betrays widespread views that perceive certain characteristics as male and associated with leadership and therefore not appropriate for women (Wajcman, 1998).

The reverse however seems to be the case for men. So, as we have
noted in Chapter 2, even though there appears to be a trend towards
the acquisition and performance of female qualities in the workplace, Swan (2006a) observes that this tends to benefit men rather
than women. Greater social value is attached to an individual male's
ability to develop and utilise feminine qualities. Coleman's study of
gender and head teachers notes that the stereotype of women as soft
and caring and men as tough and dominant can be counterproductive
for women aspiring to leadership 'as it may be assumed that they
will not be as good at leadership as aspiring men' (2005a: 2). As we
have observed in our examination of the literature in Chapter 1,
Billing and Alvesson (2000) note a trend to promote qualities and
characteristics less associated with masculinity in their summary of
developments in the leadership literature. They go on to highlight
how characteristics associated with femininity have previously
barred women from entering managerial roles. Subscribing to
gender as operating at an individual level however, essentially serves
to occlude the relationships leaders have with their workplace and
social context. Thus, the attribution of particular traits and characteristics might rather be seen as emerging from and given meaning
by their social context.

Therefore in order to debate the extent to which gender matters
in women's leadership and the impact of gender on learning
leadership, we turn to what Wharton (2005) identifies as contextual
approaches to gender. These approaches include an understanding
of gender being created through social interaction, for instance,
men and women interact in ways that are deemed to be appropriate
to their gender, such as men using sexual banter in the workplace
(Collinson and Hearn, 1996). Contextual approaches to gender also
encompass gender being understood as embedded in and reproduced
through social practices and structures and organisational and
institutional cultures. Wajcman's (1998) research on how gender is
reproduced in the workplace for example, argues that both formal
and informal organisational decision-making processes such as
recruitment, promotion and selection are based on assumptions
about gender. Gatrell and Swan (2008) in their work on gender and
diversity use the term gendered processes to refer to such practices.
Such gendered processes include the 'concrete formal and informal
activities and events in the workplace, what people say and do,

and how they think' (p. 38), for instance, formal and informal organisational activities such as promotional procedures, decision-making structures, formal and informal networks.

In the following section we provide examples from a range of studies, as referred to earlier, including the interviews discussed in Chapter 3 from our own study to illuminate how women's accounts of leadership reveal an understanding of gender as created and reproduced through social interaction and social processes and practices.

In our discussion of gender using Wharton's (2005) contextual approaches, we employ the term 'doing gender' to explore gender being created through social interaction and we use Gatrell and Swan's (2008) term of 'gendered processes' to examine gender being embedded in and reproduced through social practices, structures and organisational cultures. We attend to each of these in turn but in recognition of overlaps and linkages between the two.

In our first section, 'Doing Gender', we focus in particular on what we might term micro processes, that is, social interaction such as conversations and dialogue. We illustrate this by going on to explore the expectations and perceptions of women leaders as identified by their telling of their experiences. Finally in this section we illuminate how taking Wharton's (2005) understanding of gender created through social interaction highlights the relationship between gender, power and leadership (Fletcher, 2004).

In our second section on 'Gendered Processes' we move from the micro and the interactional – of how gender gets reproduced through conversation – to the macro and the organisational – of how gender gets reproduced through different organisational processes – for example, organisational decision-making processes such as promotion and selection. Here we examine how women's accounts of their leadership experience highlight for us a range of assumptions underpinning organisational processes that lead to what we call an opaqueness that prejudices women in leadership roles. Our examination of the organisational leads us to observe that women are often subject to what we term gender manoeuvres where women are manoeuvred into roles that are seen as suitable for their gender. We then go on to explore women leader's networks in a section entitled, 'It's who you know...'. We conclude the discussion by illuminating the key strands of our thinking in order to reflect on what might be the implications of our analysis.

A contextual approach to gender: Doing gender

In her description of contextual approaches Wharton (2005) describes an approach to understanding gender that views it as being created through social interaction. Here, men and women interact in a way that is seen as appropriate to their gender, that is, they 'do' gender. One example is the use of what Collinson and Hearn (1996) label heterosexual and homosexual subtext. This alludes to interactional practices in the workplace such as sexual banter, harassment and flirtation that are part of the social fabric of the organisation and that construct women in a way that keeps them subordinated. West and Zimmerman (2005) argue that women are assessed within normative ideas of what is appropriate behaviour for their sex. Such an evaluation may find women in leadership roles 'out of place' (p. 77). In our study Tanni Grey Thompson, for example, related that some people voiced expectations that she would not want to compete to the same extent as prior to her daughter's birth. A further example from our research is provided by Judith Donovan when she recalls her experience of joining a catalogue company and was told that although she was doing good work she could not, as a woman, expect to rise to management levels. Such accounts highlight how women leaders can clash with normative ideas of what is generally considered to be appropriate behaviour for women. These interactions might be interpreted as examples of how there are particular normative ideas of what is generally considered to be appropriate behaviour for women, that they should, for example, put their family before their ambition or not expect to have the same ambition as men.

Indeed Eagly and Carli (2007: 137) state these kind of interactions as the norm and that they can be traced to how people think:

> Predictably, people think about leadership mainly in masculine terms. These mental associations about leadership not only shape stereotypes about leaders but also influence organizational norms and practices.

They go on to say that conceiving leadership in masculine terms can mean that women encounter double standards in terms of what they are expected to achieve. Drawing on work by Martin (2003) they give the example of women attorneys in US law firms who have to work to higher standards than men to gain seniority:

> to convince her colleagues that she is worthy of advancement, a woman is often held to standards that are set higher for women than for men. (Eagly and Carli, 2007: 139)

An example of how double standards are then articulated through interactions is demonstrated by an account from Dianne Thompson, Veuve Clicquot Award winner in research by Vinnicombe and Bank (2003). She notes that during an interview at a multi-national corporation;

> When I was actually interviewed for the job they said to me that to be treated equally I had to be at least 10 per cent better than men (p. 244)

Expectations of women and how women are supposed to perform and behave are shown here to be different to expectations of men's performance and behaviour. Ruth Simmons, the first African American woman to head an Ivy League University (Brown University) in the United States of America in 2001, offers a salient example. In an interview with Alive Kessler-Harris and Cora Kaplan (Hartman, 1999) she recalls that when she was graduating only men were attributed with the term 'brilliant'. This was, she attests, part of preparing men for work and for greater achievements than women. She says:

> When I went to college, I went to a co-ed school where the whole notion was that it was more important for men to succeed and achieve than women. It was clear in my college that men were being prepared for something special and that whether in academics or extracurricular activity, it was appropriate for men to dominate. I had learned as a child to defer to men – to their wishes and to their goals – and I carried that with me into college. While learning about my own possibilities, I was not internalizing those as yet. I was just able to store all this information from other cultures and other people's lives. I can still remember the men who graduated with me in high school and how I thought

of them as much more brilliant than I or other girls. In fact, one didn't use the term brilliant for women, and I certainly didn't think of myself as brilliant, even though as I look back, I was one of the brightest kids in my class. In a way, I suppose I thought back then that I did not deserve to be called 'brilliant'.

(Hartman 1999: 245)

In this account, attributing academic brilliance to men then had the effect of positioning the women socially and intellectually as second class in spite of their actual ability. Not attributing brilliance to women has the effect here of making explicit to Ruth Simmons that this brilliance is a characteristic that she as a woman doesn't have. We might then interpret this kind of interaction where, in attributing to men a particular characteristic it is denied to women and thus works to cement women's position as socially and intellectually inferior to men. In this way we might conclude that such interactions may have the effect of stunting women's ambition so that they don't feel they can or should aspire to leadership roles.

Expectations and perceptions of women leaders

A perception that women have less ambition than men and are therefore not expected to achieve, necessarily impacts upon women leaders throughout their working lives. Women leaders' accounts illustrate this perception, from schooldays as highlighted by Ruth Simmons' account above, to when women enter the workplace and through to their continuing career development. Expectations of women leaders, the women observed, are also inflected by class and race. As we highlight in Chapter 3, Sayeeda Khan noted that as the daughter of middle-class parents she was expected to go to university, whereas there were fewer expectations of girls from less affluent backgrounds.

We also noted in Chapter 3 how May Blood's account of working in a linen mill provides an example of how expectations were shaped by her working-class background and the dominant culture operating in the mill. For example, she recalls that in spite of the mill workforce being predominantly women the men held the strategic positions. On her desire for more responsibility, she remembers her supervisor saying that he had given her a job, what more did she want. She concludes, 'as a woman my expectations were too low'.

Within her account is the assumption that women were not expected to achieve or to want to achieve, and that this was presented as a fait accompli, something not to be argued with and that was beyond change and negotiation. This in turn, as May Blood recalls, had the effect of limiting her own expectations. Indeed, this account strongly suggests an expectation that as a woman she should be grateful to have been given any employment at all.

May Blood recognises the socially conferred lower status of women and of women leaders when she recalls her role as a community worker. Part of her role involved identifying issues of importance to women and children across the two sectarian communities – the Roman Catholic community and the Protestant community. As we noted in Chapter 3, working with both communities was potentially dangerous as this meant physically moving in and out of different areas that strongly opposed each other.

May Blood however, found that being female enabled her to move between the two communities. She recalls:

> I wasn't considered orange *(Protestant and Loyalist)* or green *(Roman Catholic and Republican)*, I was only a woman *(our explanation in italics)*.

Similar to her account of setting up a political party, presented in Chapter 3, this account also presents a perception of women as holding little importance in either community. Thus, although this perception afforded May Blood an advantage – the ability to move freely – it also presents a view of women as having little value or influence.

Doing gender, doing power and doing leadership

A focus on gender as created through social interaction as in the accounts above also illuminates links between what Fletcher (2004) refers to as 'doing gender', 'doing power' and 'doing leadership'. May Blood's account of wanting more responsibility paints a picture of how she and her female colleagues are considered, because of their gender, to be inappropriate candidates for responsible work. They are subordinated and with little agency, while the male supervisors are seen as being appropriate choices for positions of responsibility, as superior and as having greater agency. The account given by Ruth Simmons of the label 'brilliance' being reserved for her fellow male graduates also illuminates the interplay of gender, power and leadership. This example highlights the positioning of the women students as academically less worthy and places them in a position of inferiority in aspiring to jobs of responsibility. The male students however, by being able to achieve the accolade of brilliance, are presented as having leadership potential.

A further example of how doing gender, doing power and doing leadership are interlinked is provided by an account from Baroness Patricia Scotland in an interview with The Guardian newspaper (2008). During her interview, which addresses in part her route to becoming the first attorney general of England, Wales and Northern Ireland, she talks about encountering people's assumptions that being a barrister was not for her. In this extract from the interview, the interviewer records:

> She is, she says, used to confronting other people's assumptions about her "I was once told people of my sort would find [*becoming a barrister*] difficult. So I said, 'What sort is that exactly?' when they stumbled I said, 'Oh, you mean socialists? Do you mean Catholics? People from Walthamstow? People who haven't been educated in private schools? What sort?' "I knew exactly what they were talking about," Scotland says and laughs. "I thought, 'Let the embarrassment be yours, not mine.' People are frightened of what they don't know."

Her example highlights interlinked issues between power, race, gender and leadership. By aspiring to a senior leadership role she is attempting to enter what is traditionally a white and male environment. Being black and being a woman in a position of authority or in aspiring to a position of authority places her as a space invader (Puwar, 2004), that is someone who does not conform to the norm in a particular environment where it is more common, for example, to be white and male. In this way, her being a black woman who is seeking to achieve a position of authority might be interpreted as presenting a challenge to the established power base.

This vivid example of the interconnectedness between gender, power and leadership is further illustrated by looking at social interactions with reference to the ways in which women are expected to behave when they have family responsibilities. Gatrell (2005, 2008) notes in her research on working mothers that women are held primarily accountable for family responsibilities including the care of children and domestic duties. This then puts women into the position of not doing gender appropriately if they take on other responsibilities, which in turn singles them out as different and 'other'.

In her full report detailing her study of UK head teachers for example, Coleman (2005b) noted that discriminatory comments recalled by her interviewees often related to their role within the family. She offers two relevant examples, a primary school head teacher being asked how her role fitted with her being a mother to four young children, and a secondary head teacher recalling how she was asked at an interview what her husband would say if she was appointed. Here, perceptions of women entering leadership roles are seen to be shaped by what is expected of their gender, which is socially deemed to mainly consist of caring for the home and family. While it is now illegal in the UK to question women about their domestic situations it is not clear that this makes much difference to perceptions of what women should do, for example, as Gatrell and Swan (2008) note, there is a gap between policy and practice. Conversely, unless women are seen to not have any family responsibilities, they are unlikely to achieve positions of authority. For instance, citing examples of women in law firms Eagly and Carli (2007) note that those in leadership roles are expected to work excessively long hours, a demand that is not compatible with family responsibilities. By working long hours and not taking on family responsibilities, these women do not behave in ways that are commensurate with expectations of women doing gender. Their behaviour might then be seen as more in keeping with masculine ways of behaving, which then sets them apart as different and not engaging in appropriate behaviour. Taken at face value, these women are therefore in a no-win position. Either they do gender and so do not fulfil expectations of leadership or they fulfil the expectations by working long hours but in so doing do not fulfil what is expected of their gender.

Each of these examples of social interaction illuminates the complexity of gender and how it is bound up with issues of power and leadership. This complex interlinking of gender, power and leadership not only raises significant barriers for women in achieving positions of authority but also perpetuates the myth of gender neutrality. As noted earlier Acker (1990, 1995) describes such expectations as evidence that organisations are not gender neutral, but rather typically favour a male employee who has minimal obligations beyond the workplace.

A contextual approach to gender: Gendered processes

The impact of gender upon women's leadership practice and their learning of leadership can be analysed in more depth by exploring a further contextual understanding of gender as embedded in and reproduced through social practices and structures (Wharton, 2005).

This understanding of gender foregrounds what Gatrell and Swan describe as 'gendered processes' (2008: 38). As we noted in the introduction to this chapter, Gatrell and Swan describe such processes as the 'concrete formal and informal activities and events in the workplace; what people say and do, and how they think' (ibid.). This description has distinct overlaps with the notion of gender being created through social interaction. However while the previous discussion focused on the interactional, in this section we focus on the organisational. By the organisational we mean the formal and informal workplace and organisational practices, structures and processes such as promotion, decision-making, recruitment and selection and gaining access to positions of influence.

While the previous section focused particularly on how expectations and perceptions of women might be deemed appropriate or inappropriate for women and how these were played out, this section takes a closer look at how formal and informal organisational structures, practices and procedures impact upon women's leadership. We have already noted how workplace expectations are produced and reproduced through gendered processes, for example, working excessively long hours. Such norms, we observe, assume an 'ideal' typically male worker with minimal domestic commitments and thus work to penalise women who traditionally have additional domestic responsibilities. In this way we can see how expectations and perceptions of women are inextricably intertwined with workplace practices and procedures. This intertwining of expectations, perceptions and gendered processes is particularly stark in accounts from women leaders of seeking promotion, and of gaining access to positions of influence.

The opaqueness of gendered processes

In our study of women leaders Rennie Fritchie talked about her experience of seeking a managerial role in her early career. She found that there was no formal route for her to progress. Although this lack of opportunity wasn't explicitly articulated, the managerial environment was largely male and so by implication managerial roles were associated with men. This environment had the effect of marginalising her chances of gaining formal promotion. What is particularly striking about this example is the opaqueness of organisational processes. Here, there was a distinct lack of clarity about whether managerial positions are open to all and how a woman might gain advancement. This opaqueness is further illustrated by Eagly and Carli's (2007) work. In their exploration of barriers to women's advancement they note that women may not be given challenging enough work that will enable them to move into senior roles. They cite an example from Erkut (2001) of a female executive who was prevented from progressing her career by being denied the opportunity to travel:

> She should have been the director of the office in about 1985 but what happened was that they brought some man in from another place and put him above her. They gave as a reason that she didn't travel. They never let her travel.
>
> (Eagly and Carli, 2007: 149)

This account indicates that by being denied the opportunity to travel, the female executive was not given the opportunity to take on a more responsible position. The account highlights the opaqueness of organiational practices in that while there is an implicit assumption that the organisation did not want the female executive to travel, the reason given is in contention. The organisation states that the woman did not want to travel whereas the account here presents the reason as being that the organisation would not allow the woman to travel. For the woman relating this account the rationale is not explicit but clearly gendered. The message is that because she is a woman the opportunity to travel is not available, and this has the subsequent effect of blocking her progress to more senior roles.

This opaqueness may be due to differing assumptions, for example, assumptions about the domestic sphere and either not being able, or wanting, to take time away from the family. We would also suggest that the opaqueness is also due in part to the taken for granted assumption that leadership is the prerogative of men. An account provided by Jocelyne Bell Burnell, President of the Institute of Physics (UK), is helpful in exemplifying this argument. In an interview with the BBC (2008), she talks about the controversy surrounding the award of the Nobel Prize for Physics in 1974. As a student undertaking her doctorate she discovered pulsars, which are essentially radio waves emitted by stars. This was hailed as significant progress in the field of radio astrophysics and the discovery was nominated for a Nobel prize. Despite this, the prize was awarded to her supervisor rather than to her in spite of her being responsible for the discovery of pulsars. Reflecting on this she observes that this was how things were:

> The picture used to be there was a senior person, inevitably male, probably wearing a white coat and under this senior person there were a load of minions who did what he said and weren't expected to think, and with that picture of how science was conducted then it's quite reasonable that the boss man gets the prizes.

This, alongside the other examples given above, serves to highlight how leadership has a cultural and historical association with the male. While things have progressed since the 1970s and 1980s – for instance, Bell Burnell acknowledges that more recently Nobel prizes have been awarded to both the student and the supervisor – such cultural and historical associations have long term effects at an individual and a collective level. The accounts given here illustrate that there are individual consequences arising from gendered processes in gaining access to positions of influence and in furthering individual careers. With a tacit acceptance in society that men's careers will take priority over the careers of women, Coleman's work (2005b: 14) observes that these individual consequences relate however to broader social concerns. How gendered processes have wider social effects can be exemplified by an account from May Blood. As outlined in Chapter 3 in her interview with us, May Blood talks about establishing the Women's Coalition Party in order to gain representation for women's issues at government level. There were, she states, in 1996, no women represented at the talks which were to lead to plans for devolved government in Northern Ireland. She recalls:

> I found myself in 1996 being one of the founder members of the Northern Ireland Women's Coalition Party … and that was

specifically set up to put women through talks. ... With women working in other parties they were always going to be relegated to the second division and a group of us made up our minds it was going to be women at the front table.

Her account of how she became a founder member of the Women's Coalition Party acknowledges leadership in Northern Irish political parties as male-dominated. With only men at the front table, women and women's issues would effectively be excluded from important decision-making. These accounts of how leadership is typically viewed as male not only illustrate what Knights and Kerfoot label (2004) the 'gender binary', that is, the division between men and women, but also serve to highlight how women are viewed as not 'natural' leaders. This has resonance with work by Jackie Ford (2006). In her study of male and female managers in the UK public sector she notes that the role of leader was largely understood as hegemonic and masculine resulting in men being viewed as 'the "natural" inhabitants of organizational life', while women remained 'out of place' (Ford, 2006: 81). While men therefore remain dominant in leadership, this reinforces the accepted norm of leadership as masculine and as such women remain marginalised and viewed as different to the norm.

Gender manoeuvres

Women seen as being out of place (Ford, 2006) is also manifest in the positions into which women are recruited in organisations and the roles which they play. Women are often, we contend, subject to what we call gender manoeuvres. That is, women are manoeuvred into particular roles that are deemed appropriate for their gender. In Chapter 2 we discuss for example, the terms glass ceiling and glass cliffs in the context of our exploration of stereotypes and visual imagery of women. We note in Chapter 2 how research has observed a tendency within organisations to block women from moving into senior positions (glass ceilings) (cf. Meyerson and Fletcher, 2000). Or, where women do rise to the top to assign to them roles that are particularly challenging and have a significant risk of failure, therefore effectively positioning them on what has been termed a glass cliff (Ryan and Haslam, 2005; 2007).

A further example of what we might term gender manoeuvres is the tendency for women to be filtered into particular positions and occupations that might be deemed more appropriate to what are viewed as feminine characteristics and qualities. For instance, Vinnicombe and Bank (2003) note how organisations may encourage women into positions in personnel and human resources that typically may have less authority and a more reduced status than generalist managerial positions. Both their and our study include a number of examples of this gender manoeuvring on the part of women leaders who began their careers in the 1970s and 1980s. One of Vinnicombe and Bank's (2003) interviewees, for instance, recalls being told by a large UK organisation that women could only rise to the top of the company if they were in Personnel. Judith Donovan's account in Chapter 3 of being a graduate trainee with an automobile engineering company during her early career recalls a similar experience. In this account she remembers that there was a surplus of marketing graduate trainees and so they asked the women to work in personnel instead.

While this kind of manoeuvring by organisations may be less blatant with the introduction of equal opportunity legislation, it still has as noted in our discussion about the opaqueness of gendered processes, resonance for women leaders today.

In our study, Rennie Fritchie observes in her interview that senior women today are less likely to be at the top of organisations because they are more likely to be employed within Human Resource Departments:

> I think it is not unusual that we don't find women at the top of the businesses because when they do go into the commercial environment they tend to go down the HR route, and very many organizations don't have HR directors on their boards, and if they get to being a business of size [and] then they want a HR director on board they go out and get a man.

Here Rennie Fritchie presents the Human Resources function as noted for being primarily staffed by women. She observes that when Human Resources is represented at board level it then typically becomes a male role, thereby implying that women are not worthy of board level appointments. Levinson's research (1996) helps us explore this notion of gender and roles further. In his study of women's lives he raises the concept of 'genderized occupations' which he identifies as occupations where either men or women are dominant (p. 49). Female-dominated occupations, for instance, caring professions such as nursing and teaching, are viewed as female, he argues, because they are associated with traditionally feminine qualities such as nurturing and looking after others. Levinson notes that these kind of occupations have particular characteristics that render them less important. They are, for example, often underpaid compared to other professions such as engineering or manufacturing which are male-dominated. Levinson also notes that when women do gain senior roles, the roles typically have less authority than equivalent roles in organisations where men hold the top jobs. Furthermore, Levinson observes that female-dominated organisations become 'feminized' (1996: 417). As feminised occupations, he argues, they embody women's work and thus have less value and worth as an occupation. This in turn makes them less attractive to men thereby perpetuating such occupations as female-dominated.

We have noted that gender manoeuvres are in evidence in multiple ways including positioning women into roles that are high risk and filtering them into roles associated with what are viewed as feminine characteristics. This may have the effect of women being socialised into such roles and so perpetuating gender manoeuvring. On the other hand, the effects of such gender manoeuvres may be that women's leadership can become perceived within a static and biological frame of gender. By this we mean an understanding of gender that divides men from women in terms of perceived different qualities and characteristics that are either masculine or feminine. As such, women leaders continue to be viewed as 'unnatural inhabitants' of senior roles with little chance of progression (Ford, 2006). Viewing gender as a fundamental organising principle however, enables us to examine organisational processes more optimistically and to illuminate and challenge such positioning and the processes and activities that enable it.

It's who you know

The significance of gender in women's leadership is also made apparent by exploring women leaders' networks. The accounts from the women in our study that we highlighted in Chapter 3 indicate that women leaders' networks are multi-layered, dynamic and shifting to meet the needs of women leaders as they develop their careers. Networks, we observed, are important in supporting, motivating and sustaining women in their leadership practice. Current research notes the effect of gender on networks (Ibarra, 1997; Singh et al. 2006). Eagly and Carli (2007: 139), for example, state 'gender affects social capital; women usually have less of it'. By social capital they refer to the access to and membership of a range of professional networks and relationships. Timberlake's examination of social capital and the workplace (2005: 35) observes the effect of a lack of social capital in relation to career progression for women. She says:

> women are hindered in their efforts to achieve career advancement and its associated benefits due to their inability to access social capital, a valuable organizational commodity and source of the knowledge, resources and networks that are essential for career development and maturation.

Social capital and access to important networks and relationships is then cumulative and as Timberlake suggests, 'the components of trust, communication, rich networks and shared norms increase with each successive interaction' (2005: 35). Timberlake (2005) goes on to note that it is social capital rather than human capital, an individual's experience, knowledge, skills and education, that provides greater opportunity for achievement at senior levels.

Timberlake's (ibid.) study of the literature on social networks at work goes on to outline three possible reasons why women do not have equal access to social capital: women feeling uncomfortable in male-dominated networks, women being viewed as 'outsiders' and men seeking to maintain their dominance of networks.

First, she suggests, men and women can feel uncomfortable in networks that are dominated by the other sex and this leads them to either being excluded or avoiding getting involved. Women who find themselves in the minority in professional networks may then seek to develop alternative networks. Ibarra (1997) observes that one strategy to overcome this lack of comfort is to look beyond the organisation in order to build social capital. The accounts of women leaders in our study illustrate this. For example, Sayeeda Khan talks about the importance of building networks and alliances and has built up a wide-ranging professional network that draws on a range of men and women from a variety of organisations. A further way in which women seek to build social capital is in developing women-only networks. Rennie Fritchie's account of her women-only network and how it supports her illuminates the importance of being able to connect to people whose experiences are similar. However, research indicates that networks that don't include men are typically perceived as less influential (Brass, 1985). With men having more senior roles, women-only networks can serve to perpetuate women's lack of social capital (Eagly and Carli, 2007). Where women do gain access, Kanter (1977) raises the issue of tokenism. Her research suggests that being in the minority within social networks may push women into stereotypical roles, such as those described in Chapter 2. For instance, in order to be accepted within a male-dominated network, women may feel the need to take on masculine attributes as represented by the image of the Iron Maiden, or to sacrifice their own needs for the common good of the network as represented by the image of the Selfless Heroine.

The second issue raised by Timberlake (2005) is that with many networks dominated by men, women may be viewed as 'outsiders' which prevents them from gaining access. We have noted earlier how Ford's (2006) study of public sector workers saw women as 'out of place' in senior roles. Being in the minority means being outside of the leadership norm and therefore women may not be seen as insiders and part of the in crowd, but as noted by Timberlake (2005), viewed as outsiders. As outsiders women therefore do not have the legitimacy of insiders.

Ibarra (1997) notes the importance of sponsorship as a way of gaining legitimacy. In our research May Blood and Betty Boothroyd's accounts of how they see it as part of their role to encourage other women might be interpreted as a form of such sponsorship, thereby enabling those in more junior positions to gain legitimacy and there-fore access to senior networks.

The third reason considered by Timberlake is that men, as the dominant group may seek to maintain that dominance within social networks by excluding women. Eagly and Carli (2007) observe that such exclusion is manifest in organisational norms and practices, through activities such as after hours socialising. This can be prob-lematic for women on a number of levels. As Singh et al. (2006) note in their exploration of women in formal corporate networks, those with family responsibilities can be particularly disadvantaged when it comes to after hours socialising which may result, for example, in exchange of important information. Women may be further disadvantaged as male-dominated networks can be based on masculine activities such as playing golf or going to football matches. In our interview with Dawn Gibbins, she refers to the dominance of male social networks in doing business as a reason why women aren't gaining leadership roles:

> But this going to the pub to do deals, this you know, old boys' network, it is still there. The golf course, the rugby, the football, I'm afraid it is still there and very strong and you know, lots of decisions are made there, when the women aren't there. So ... we've got to look at different ways of doing business haven't we?

This quotation highlights both the importance of such social networks, for example, as a place where deals might be done and decisions made, and the way in which gender affects entrance to and membership of such networks. Indeed, we might observe that each of these points raised by Timberlake (2005) is not distinct but rather have a cumulative effect in hindering women's access to top roles. For example, Eagly and Carli (2007: 145) quote a Chief Executive Officer from a study by Heffernan (2004):

> It's hard to resist the feeling that at meetings, at conferences, on golf courses, women are gatecrashers.

This feeling of being a gatecrasher serves to illustrate how women might feel as outsiders, particularly with a focus on masculine activities. This feeling of being an outsider in turn can serve to make women feel uncomfortable and exclude themselves from social networks, which in turn perpetuates a lack of access for women to social capital. The overall paucity of women leaders means that there is no equivalent to the old boy network (Vinnicombe and Bank, 2003), which has the corresponding effect of fewer role models and mentors in influential networks from whom aspiring women leaders may gain sponsorship. This then equates to fewer opportunities for women to learn from the experiences of other women on how to deal with the barriers raised by gendered processes, thus compromising the ability for women to gain or sustain leadership positions.

Conclusions

Our analysis of the impact of gender on women's leadership illuminates that gender is not, in the words of Joan Acker, 'an addition to ongoing processes, conceived as gender neutral. Rather it is an integral part of those processes, which cannot be properly understood without an analysis of gender' (1990: 146). Thus, gender is a fundamental organising element in the everyday practices, processes and interactions of working life. In this chapter we have used accounts from a range of studies of women leaders including our own to exemplify what Wharton (2005) calls contextual approaches to gender. In particular, we have focused on 'doing gender' and on 'gendered processes'. In our discussion of doing gender we have emphasised how gender is created through social interaction, raising expectations and giving rise to perceptions that men and women will behave in ways that are seen to be appropriate to their gender. We have then turned our attention from the interactional to the organisational with a focus on gendered processes, that is, the organisational processes, procedures and practices such as decision-making, networks and career promotion and how they impact women leaders. We have recognised that while our discussion separates doing gender and gendered processes, they are nonetheless inextricably intertwined. Here our analysis illustrates how notions of appropriate behaviour for women and men are entangled within gendered processes. For example, how expectations of what women might achieve are framed by processes that filter women into particular occupations, or conversely how social networks exclude with a focus on traditionally male-dominated activities. We would argue therefore, that while it is helpful to be able to point to accounts and experiences that highlight different aspects of doing gender and gendered processes, their very entanglement is significant in that it serves to illuminate the multiple and complex ways in which gender operates.

The accounts of women leaders illustrate that having to deal with the norms that are produced and reproduced through social interaction hinders women's leadership in different ways including through

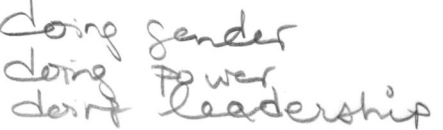

the development of double standards, the lesser expectations placed on women and the inferior positioning of women. These accounts have also highlighted that doing gender is inextricably linked with doing power and doing leadership. Within a social frame that privileges the male, this triumvirate serves to marginalise women and their experiences.

Our analysis of gendered processes enabled us to explore such marginalisation further and illuminated how gendered processes have the effect of positioning women leaders as different and as outsiders. In particular we observed the opaqueness of gendered processes, that while the effect of organisational processes and practices are explicit in their exclusion and marginalisation of women leaders, the rationale of such processes and practices remains clouded. We also identified the practice of gender manoeuvres, where women are manoeuvred into particular roles seen as appropriate to their gender. Finally our discussion of gendered processes examined gender and networks and how women leaders have less social capital than men leaders.

Our discussion, illuminated by women leaders' accounts has thus illustrated that gender has a significant and fundamental impact on women leaders. We note that this impact operates at individual and collective levels. For example, a consideration of the opaqueness of gendered processes led us to consider how leadership comes to be associated with the male, and how this is a cultural and historical association. As such we argue that it affects women as individuals, for instance, in terms of their own career development, as well as affecting the collective as in the sustained exclusion of women at senior organisational levels. Our focus on gender manoeuvres showed the individual impact of women being filtered into particular roles. It also observed the impact at the collective level of 'feminising' roles and occupations which then are accorded lesser status, thus perpetuating the male/female divide. In our examination of networks and gender we argued that as a consequence of having less social capital there is both less opportunity for individual advancement and collectively fewer opportunities for learning among women leaders.

Our analysis of the extent to which gender impacts upon women's leadership therefore concludes that gender is fundamental in organising leadership. We cannot consider leadership in isolation from gender and indeed to do so is to deny not only a critical understanding of leadership but a significant body of women leaders' experiences. By recognising gender as a fundamental organising element, there are however significant implications on a number of levels. What then are the implications for women being identified as leaders? How does this analysis inform leadership learning? What then are the implications for the development of women leaders? We turn to these questions in the following chapters.

Part III Progressing Women's Leadership

5
Women's Leadership Identity

> And in this job I do have to try to please a lot of
> people. I try and appeal to a lot of people to do
> fund raising, and to try and keep the membership
> happy and try and keep the staff happy, but also
> try and be challenging. And I do get patronised
> by various people. Of course I do, you know. I am
> youngish – although people say that I look younger
> than I am and that doesn't help – a few grey hairs
> won't hurt.
>
> —Sayeeda Khan (Senior leader in a UK charitable
> organisation)

Our focus in this chapter is to draw on the analyses we presented
in previous chapters and consider the implications these raise for
women's leadership identity. We explore why women are not readily
identified as leaders particularly when, as the quote from Sayeeda
Khan above illustrates, your appearance contrasts with received
understandings of what leaders look like and can elicit negative
responses. Drawing on Ashcraft and Mumby's (2004) framework the
chapter's objective is to consider how discourse organises identity.
That is, we will examine the relationship between broader societal
narratives of gender and dominant discourses in organisations and
work towards making sense of how certain discourses of leadership
identity come to be privileged. We recognise that the topic of identity
is a much contested and debated field. Alvesson, Ashcraft and
Thomas (2008) note that within organisation studies identity can be
associated with a range of organisational processes and intervention,
from company mergers and project teams through to motivation and
politics. Collinson (2003) examines the influence of organisations

on self-identity arguing that this is now more significant than religious or family influences. Kempster (2009) too observes the large volume of literature on identity but suggests that research examining processes that influence identity construction is more limited; his focus therefore is to study the becoming of leadership identity and how this is shaped within particular situations. Our concern in this chapter is to understand how certain leadership discourses are mobilised and come to be privileged. Our focus therefore is not in making sense of the development of *individual's* leadership identity per se, rather our aim is to work towards revealing dominant leadership identity discourses through leading women's narratives of their experience. In common with Alvesson, Ashcraft and Thomas (2008) we view a focus on leadership identity as one way to revitalise understandings of leadership. The women's narratives of their leadership presented in previous chapters have, for example, alerted us to the possibilities for women's leadership, particularly the significance of the individual in resisting and shaping conceptions of leadership. To support our exploration we turn to Ashcraft and Mumby's (2004) approach as it assumes that subjectivity is 'unstable, fragmented, and constructed in an ongoing and dynamic manner through various communicative practices' (p. 117). While recognising that identity regulation can be a significant form of organisational control (Alvesson and Willmott, 2002), our aim is to illustrate identity as a 'temporary, context-sensitive and evolving set of constructions, rather than a fixed and abiding essence' (Alvesson, Ashcraft and Thomas, 2008: 6) thus allowing for possibilities of resistance to taken-for-granted leadership identities.

This chapter therefore builds on discussions in previous chapters. In Chapter 4 we used the contextual approaches to gender identified by Wharton (2005) to explore whether the gender of the leaders we have been studying is significant in their experience of practising leadership. To deepen this analysis we drew on previous studies which together led to a number of observations including aware- ness of the ways in which gender positions women leaders. We argued that holding a concept of gender that sees it as fundamental to organising, managing and leading alerts us to the ways in which gender influences at many levels. For example, gender influences through various processes including organisational processes and activities, relationships and social practices more generally.

In Chapter 2 we argued that the dearth of critical examinations regarding the impact of visual images, metaphors and stereotypes has led leadership research to ignore the variety of ways in which certain portrayals of women perpetuate prejudices about women's suitability to lead. Nevertheless paying attention to seemingly routine day-to-day social practices offers, we argued, insights into the ways in which these practices help to maintain – to take just one example – the small number of women working at boardroom level.

Chapter 3 seeks to redress this balance by presenting and discussing what we term the spheres of influence of the nine women leaders in relation to their leadership learning and practice. Working with this relatively small sample of interviewees allows us to present their narratives in some depth. We use the notion of sphere of influence to organise and make sense of the breadth and depth of experience that the women leaders access in their leadership learning and practice.

As we argued in Chapter 4 gendered processes have the effect – both within the work setting as well as in society – of positioning women as leaders differently from the way in which men leaders are generally positioned. Because of certain perceptions, expectations and values embedded in social processes and practices, the way in which women are positioned has the effect of both excluding women from, and leaving them on the margins of decision making. This then makes it more difficult for women to attain leadership roles. Given the significant body of evidence illuminating the slow pace of progress towards equality that the Equality and Human Rights Commission (2008) have recently reported, alongside our own and others' in-depth analyses, in the following sections we consider the implications for women's leadership identity in the context of women's restricted participation in recognised leadership positions. The purpose of this chapter is to examine why women are not readily identified as leaders. We do this by examining the relationship between societal narratives of gender, leadership and organisation. Taken together then, Chapters 4 and 5 engage with theories arising from gender studies that articulate our concerns regarding mainstream understandings and practices of leadership.

Women's leadership: A missing identity

The process of reading women's leadership literature and our in-depth research and analysis has made us aware that textual and visual images of leadership are significant in forming understandings of who does leadership. This is particularly the case for women leaders because as Majia Holmer Nadesan and Angela Trethewey (2000) observe, for working women, 'negotiating and performing a "professional" identity is a process requiring much time, energy, and self-surveillance' (p. 223). While the focus of their study was concerned with women in corporate organisations, through the discussions in Chapters 3 and 4 in particular, we can see that women's leadership is partly dependent on others' recognition of them as leaders irrespective of the situated context. This is true of men leaders too of course, but given that professional women and women leaders in a broad range of settings are still considered 'out of place' or 'travellers in a male world' (Marshall, 1984), this remains an important topic to address.

The understanding of leadership that we have developed in this book and other papers (Elliott and Stead, 2008) challenges traditional views that draw predominantly on men leaders' experiences and so privilege heroic and masculine leadership performances (Sinclair, 2005; Ford et al., 2008). Paying attention to women's narrations of their experience reveals how their developing aspirations emerge from their social and community context, suggesting leadership to be a process that is dynamic and emerging from collective rather than individual concerns. This moves us away from leadership research that places its analytical focus on leaders' styles of leadership, and that identifies individuals' attributes as either masculine or feminine. This tendency is, as we have articulated elsewhere (Elliott and Stead, 2008), as common in postheroic leadership models as it is in traditional models, continuing the trend to depict 'women leaders as the kind of representatives of women that follow women's natural way of behaving' (Lamsa and Sintonen, 2001: 257). By contrast the understanding of gender that we explore more fully in this chapter considers gender identities as a 'discursive product or effect' (Ashcraft and Mumby, 2004: 18). From this analytic standpoint the predominant leadership identity is directed by societal narratives, and the discourse with greater institutional support will come to, as Ashcraft and Mumby (2004) phrase it, '"look" and "feel" more persuasive' (p. 18) than other discourses. For example, a white male dressed in suit and tie chatting at the water cooler with a female wearing a corporate uniform is at first glance more likely to be taken by the viewer as being senior to his female colleague. The viewer's assumption will have been guided by images and stereotypes of organisational leaders pervading social and organisational narratives. Understanding leadership identity(ies) as formed by societal narratives seeks to examine how these identities 'find life' (ibid.) in material texts such as film, literature and academic studies. This serves to remind us of the potential impact of the visual images and stereotypes we discussed in Chapter 2 which are received and referenced, either implicitly or explicitly, in everyday life by individual actors. These images and stereotypes draw on broader discourses and feed into narrative threads that can confirm institutional understandings of what leadership looks and feels like (Ashcraft and Mumby, 2004) within particular organisations, for example, the discourse of the 'heroic' leader mobilized by Ford et al.'s (2008) interviewees.

A benefit of taking this discursive approach is that it requires us to ask questions focusing on how societal narratives of gender are appropriated by individuals in certain situations, and how 'these performances preserve and/or alter the veneer of a binary gender order' (Ashcraft and Mumby, 2004: 9). In the spirit of Ashcraft and Mumby's (2004) approach to understanding the relationship between gender and organisation – what they term a communicology of organisation – our aim when discussing implications for women's leadership identity is to draw on the interpretations from previous chapters to produce an analysis that considers how understandings of women's leadership identity(ies) have 'evolved across spheres of organizing activity' (p. 132). This is not to imply that we think there is, or has been, an over-abundance of women leaders. We are instead seeking to make sense of the gendered organising of leadership identity over the last 30 to 40 years. To do this we look at women's leadership by examining how it has been formed across different areas of practice including popular culture (Chapter 2), academic literature (Chapters 1 and 4) and individual leaders' experiences (Chapters 3 and 4). In so doing, we aim to highlight the tensions between taken-for-granted micro level social practices and macro level processes of reproduction that mobilise leadership identities. In this chapter, we have chosen to place our focus on a consideration of communication activities' role in making possible identity, practices and structures because in the light of the linguistic turn[1] we recognise that not only are realities and selves expressed through communication, but they are also produced through communication (Ashcraft and Mumby, 2004).

In doing so we acknowledge that our own research: the ways in which we assembled, analysed and interpreted the material gathered and its ultimate publication in this book is itself a reflection of, and contributes to, leadership discourses.

One of the questions that has been guiding our research is: why, 34 years after the passing of the UK Sex Discrimination Act, is it that women leaders are still seen as out of place (West and Zimmerman, 2005)? As a corollary to this, when women do achieve leadership roles, why are they so often subject to negative stereotyping and their performance judged in comparison to men leaders? And why does the 'tough guy' template (Sinclair and Wilson, 2002) of leadership persist in organisational settings that are increasingly demographically diverse and so require leaders who are sensitive to differences in cultural and social contexts? We therefore suggest that it is apposite to consider how gender discourses intersect with other discourses to articulate certain gendered identities. Ashcraft and Mumby's (2004) framework offers an approach with which we can begin to make sense of how 'macro-level institutional agents … articulate certain gendered identities' and the ways in which 'social actors reproduce and/or resist these articulations in their everyday praxis and interaction' (p. 122). The framework helps us examine 'how the relationship among gender, identity, and work is subject to shifting and frequently contradictory cultural, political, and economic forces' (pp. 122–3). Macro level agents can include organisations, groups or social movements. In paying close attention to the interaction between, say, women and Northern Irish political parties we can understand how over time 'dominant groups and institutions mobilize particular meaning systems by drawing on and articulating together existing cultural discourses' (p. 122). Dawn Gibbins' reference to the dominance of male social networks in the previous chapter illustrates how social networks work either to exclude or include individuals. The strength of male-dominated networks often arises from their base in activities such as golf or attending football matches, which are socially regarded as masculine activities and whose members mirror the demography of those holding senior organisational positions.

We structure the following discussion according to Ashcraft and Mumby's (2004) framework. This maps how authors have seen or framed the relationships between discourse, organisation, gender, power and identity.

'Essential' leadership identity(ies)

In gathering together certain approaches to research and 'framing' them according to their conceptualisation of the relationship between discourse, gender and organisation, Ashcraft and Mumby (2004) describe the first of four frames as one in which gender is treated as fundamental to individual identity. While research taking this approach considers gender as socialised, individual identity is seen as relatively static and tied to one's biological sex. In this sense, this frame has resonance with Wharton's (2005) identification of approaches that view gender as operating at the individual level, for example, the literature on gender differences (Belenky et al., 1986; Gilligan, 1982; Tannen, 1990). These approaches serve to reinforce women's leadership as innately different to men, that as leaders they display characteristics and behaviours that are 'feminine'. Despite the far from conclusive empirical research that claims women leaders are, for example, more transformational (Rosener, 1990) or more nurturing (Helgsen, 1990) than men leaders, the visual imagery associated with stereotypes of women leaders suggests that leadership remains equated with traits and behaviours associated with men. Given frame one approach's lack of attention to context, it would seem to have limited potential for researchers and practitioners interested in challenging dominant leadership templates. It tends to 'underplay the production of difference' and gender difference is spoken of in 'uniform, static, ahistorical, and uncritical terms' (Ashcraft and Mumby, 2004: 7). By essentialising women and men's traits and behaviours it places the emphasis on individual tendencies rather than systemic processes thereby presenting organisations and institutions as neutral sites of interaction where difference is presented as a 'rationale for organisational control' (ibid.: 8), for example, as justification for the gendered division of labour.

Questioning the reproduction of gender identity

Common to the approaches located in frame two is an interest in questioning how gender identity is either reproduced or challenged by dominant discourses. In contrast to approaches under frame one where 'gender organizes discourse' (ibid.: 3) and so examine how gender identity is expressed at work, research located under frame two examines the organisational formation of gender. Work on the 'doing' of gender (West and Zimmerman, 1987; West and Fenstermaker, 1995;

Fenstermaker and West, 2002) that conceptualises gender as situated, as something we do in relation to dominant gender discourses, offers an example of approaches that ask us to examine how women do leadership in different settings. In frame two Ashcraft and Mumby (2004) place work which claims 'that the performance of professional identity entails the symbolic and material manipulation of sexed bodies' (p. 10). This work is therefore concerned to reveal discursive practices, for example, formal and informal stories about maternity leave (Ashcraft, 1999; J. Martin, 1990), women's reproductive capacity (Gatrell, 2004) or their age (Trethewey, 2001) that discipline working women. Rather than ignoring or placing less emphasis on the material, 'these works demonstrate how discursive struggles translate into corporeal practices and effects, as well as how the body becomes a potent symbolic resource for identity formation' (p. 11). May Blood for example, 'does' a particular feminine identity of the socially and politically invisible woman when crossing the Northern Ireland peace line, but 'does' another identity in her work as a trade union representative in a linen mill. Baroness Blood's demonstration of her awareness of the 'situated social scripts to which we hold one another accountable' (ibid.: 12) sheds light on the ways in which macro discourses constitute gender. Her presence as a woman in traditionally male-dominated settings disrupts what are generally considered to be male activities. To borrow a theatrical metaphor, organisations under the understandings positioned under frame two 'emerge as a fairly firm stage – or sometimes, as a changing unfinished set – that establishes preferences and boundaries for gender identity performance' (ibid.: 13). That is, organisations positioned under this frame do not in themselves appear as active producers of meaning.

Constantly organising identity

Within approaches placed under frame three, by contrast, organisation emerges as a 'precarious social construction, more unfinished set than fixed stage' (ibid.). Identity is actively (en)gendered by organisation(s), so any one leader's identity 'becomes an organisational process and outcome' (ibid.: 13). Organisation thus produces, and is a product of, gender discourses; it 'guides interaction, predisposing and rewarding members to practice in particular ways' (ibid.). Research working from within this understanding therefore seeks to reveal how certain masculinities come to be embedded in organisational forms, and 'how these forms tacitly direct member interaction (and therefore institutionalise gender inequality) and translate into tangible consequences for women and men' (ibid.: 15). With its focus on the workplace, approaches placed under frame three are especially concerned with examining how identities are produced by 'institutionalized narratives about how people and labor should be arranged and carried out' (ibid.: 17); organisations are therefore not seen as gender-neutral. So organisations might introduce diversity awareness training but this alone will be insufficient in shifting power relationships. Conceiving organisational processes and practices as formed by 'discourse communities' that privilege certain conceptions of gender, provides a perspective on organisational forms that helps us to begin to recognise how certain identities attain more power than others within day-to-day interactions. This can become particularly visible when individuals puncture others' assumptions about their position within institutions. Examples we referred to in the previous chapter including Baroness Scotland's challenge to the dominant discourse concerning the identity of barristers that she encountered in everyday conversations, and Ruth Simmons' awareness that only male graduates were identified as brilliant, draws our attention to the relationship between macro and micro layers of discourse. It illuminates the power of macro level discourses within organisational settings and how these reproduce masculine and feminine identities in the often fleeting daily interactions in which individual actors engage.

Gender discourse and identity beyond the workplace

One of the limitations that we see in relation to the majority of studies that Ashcraft and Mumby (2004) position in frame three is that they tend not to look beyond work organisations when examining the relation between gender and identity. Throughout our research we have been acutely aware that an examination of women's leadership will achieve greater explanatory power by taking into account broader societal narratives of gender that are possibly at their most accessible in the mainstream media and in various forms of popular culture (e.g. cartoons, film, lifestyle magazines), and this is the interest of approaches positioned under the fourth frame. Holmer Nadesan and Trethewey's (2000) study of the ways in which professional women both internalise and resist the discourses of the popular success-literature including the advice columns found in women's and professional trade magazines as well as books (e.g. Brooks and Brooks, 1997), throws light on the power of broader gender narratives on how women perform their identity at work. Emma Bell (2008) discusses the role of films in reinforcing the construction of working women as out of place in work organisations. In noting the congruence between empirical studies of women's work experiences and representation of these experiences in films, she nevertheless suggests that representations of working women in films might also 'be partially responsible for constituting this reality' and that the barriers to progression faced by women in organisations and management might also be 'adversely effected by the representation of working women in film' (p 159). Film therefore, can be seen as another site where the relationship between competing discourses can be observed in the struggle for dominance. Film texts can offer vivid illustrations of competing discourses at play, for as Bell (2008) observes, while film has 'been used to construct and reinforce the dominant category of "organization man" it has also been used to give voice to the subordinate category of "working woman", through representing the marginalizing and exclusionary effects of gendered organizational practices as in films such as *The Associate* (1996)[2] and *North Country* (2005)'[3] (p. 159). We should not however, think of the film viewer as a cultural dope (Garfinkel, 1967) Bell argues; rather how individual viewers/actors interpret competing discourses will be influenced by their cultural and historical context and attendant discourses. In relation to organisational texts produced for public consumption Benschop and Meihuizen's (2002) analysis of representations of gender in financial reports of 30 corporations concludes that 'male dominance in organisational arrangements and the gendered division of labour highlighted in socialist feminist theories are broadly reinforced in annual reports' (p. 632). Representations of gender are not neutral reflections of gendering process in organisations, they argue, but are 'factors which help constitute that reality' (ibid.). Ford et al. (2008) draw our attention to the role played by popular management texts in promoting certain discourses in their discussion on the rise in popularity of 'emotional intelligence' (Goleman, 1996, 2002) in management and business studies, observing how this has become a narrative thread in UK National Health Service (NHS) leadership development courses. NHS leaders are therefore encouraged to be 'nice' and to engage in certain practices such as talking openly about themselves to others and inviting others to give them feedback about their strengths and weaknesses. As Ford et al. (2008) point out: 'western culture is saturated with concepts of leadership. Leadership training programmes draw upon the libidinal energies thus aroused to persuade participants to open themselves to a new way of being, to a new identity' (p. 84). The narrative of emotions that is emerging in late-modernist organisations, of which the turn to 'niceness' constitutes one thread, contributes they suggest 'to the control of leaders through the attempt to constitute a managerial identity that is malleable and unquestioning' (p. 82). While Ford et al. (2008) draw our attention to the influence of popular management texts on leadership development interventions, Alvesson and Willmott (2002) note the various processes employed within corporate education programmes to encourage employees to adopt 'new managerial discourses into narratives of self-identity' (p. 622). Referring in particular to what they term 'discourses' of management interventions including quality management, innovation and knowledge work, Alvesson and Willmott (2002) argue that these can also be interpreted as 'expressions of an increased management interest in regulating employees' "insides" – their self-image, their feelings and identifications' (ibid.). Processes employed to facilitate this include written texts such as in-house magazines and posters, as well as induction and training programmes.

Alongside our own observations, the examples presented by these studies support the value in taking cognizance of the relationship between discourse and the material world. In so doing, we are better placed to make sense of the significance of social, cultural, political and economic forces on the relationship between gender and leadership identity. In the following section we consider what this means for women's leadership.

Towards alternative conceptions of women's leadership

In continuing the feminist project of studying and critiquing the material features of patriarchy, Ashcraft and Mumby (2004) see no contradiction in 'arguing for a material and durable social world on the one hand, and claiming that such a world is socially constructed on the other' (p. 123). Communication itself is, they propose, 'a material act. Framed materially, communication constitutes the day-to-day practices of social actors' (pp. 123–4); as social actors individuals therefore enact discourses in different social contexts. We identified above how May Blood 'does' a particular feminine identity (Fenstermaker and West, 2002; West and Fenstermaker, 1995; West and Zimmerman, 1987) of the socially and politically invisible woman when crossing the Northern Ireland peace line, but 'does' another identity in her work as a trade union representative in a linen mill. How she performs these different identities emerges from her awareness of the role of women in Northern Irish society and within the industrial workplace at particular points in time. The two examples articulated in May Blood's account of her leadership experience demonstrate how the material world of institutional and social structures and processes has been disturbed by her – as a social actor – resistance to the discourses of gender identity articulated by macro level agents. Similarly, when Rennie Fritchie describes her organisational experiences during the early years of her working life, she presents an account of how she – through her awareness of the barriers posed to women by the predominantly male managerial environment – succeeded in negotiating her way to a managerial position. She did so by disturbing the taken-for-granted institutional processes that discriminated against women's career progression. Although lacking any official opportunities, she set upon creating her own managerial role by taking on extra duties and responsibilities, finding it particularly fruitful to do so in areas that were unpopular with colleagues, such as administrative duties. Having developed a role equivalent to managerial status she gained status as a manager by presenting her Managing Director with, as she describes it, a 'fait accompli'. Taking this approach was, she asserts, the only way she would ever gain recognition in the workplace.

What May Blood's and Rennie Fritchie's reflections on their learning leadership experience so strikingly capture are their – as individual actors – ability to engage with and subsequently challenge worlds that have been socially constructed to, in this case, discriminate against women achieving positions of authority and influence. These accounts constitute just two examples that illustrate the ways in which, as Ashcraft and Mumby (2004) describe, an analytic charac-teristic of their framework, individual 'agency/identity and structure are co-constructed' (p. 115). In taking this approach, that is, by not forcing a choice between an 'essentialist focus on the enduring material conditions of oppression and a discursive, textual interest in unstable systems of meaning' (ibid.), we have the opportunity to explore the dialectical relationship between agency and structure. This creates the possibility of conceiving of leadership in alternative, more creative ways. While modernist stances on feminism have, as Ashcraft and Mumby highlight, a strong tradition in exposing the institutionalisation of patriarchy, we suggest that less analytic work in leadership research has taken place examining how individuals' understanding of (gender) discourses can lead to shifts in institutional structures and processes. Research on women's leadership in the business and organisation studies field as well as portrayals of women's leadership in the media and popular culture more broadly has, as we outline in earlier chapters, taken a somewhat pessimistic tone in its search for models of women's leadership within corporate settings. Potential women leaders are variously depicted as either being in a constant battle with invisible organisational barriers (glass ceiling), as being set up to fail (glass cliff) or as performing as men (Iron Lady). The research on glass cliffs and glass ceilings is extensive and rigorous and we do not disagree with its premises and findings. However, because the empirical location of much of this research remains the corporate setting it limits the possibilities for more creative understandings of what women's leadership, and by extension leadership more generally, could be. Hartman (1999), in her edited collection of conversations with women leaders points out that industrialised societies such as the United States and the UK tend to discount the long history of women's leadership in their homes and communities. As she observes:

> throughout the long span of human history, men and women alike have done most of their leading from the base of their immediate households and extended kinship networks, rather than from the many religious, political, economic, and cultural institutions that have come to be erected outside those networks.
>
> (p. 3)

By ignoring this rich history of leadership and by placing leadership firmly as a concern of business and corporations, she argues that we erroneously place women as emerging leaders. Studies of women leaders therefore must look beyond the corporate world, Hartman (1999) argues, not only to address what she labels 'the "supposed" anomaly that is women's leadership' (p. 12), but also to enrich and expand leadership studies as both multi- and inter-disciplinary.

Moving women's leadership forward

Nevertheless there do exist studies that examine women's leadership outside the particular institutional structures and mechanisms of corporate organisations that act as a critical mirror to question the ways in which who a leader is, what (s)he looks like and how leadership is practised have been symbolically and materially represented and organised. The research literature that studies the experiences of African-American women during the civil rights movement in the 1960s describes how those without access to traditional forms of power rose to positions of leadership. Barnett (1993: 163) describes the 'invisibility' of southern black women leaders who 'were seldom recognised as leaders', but who nevertheless were the ones who often 'initiated protest, formulated strategies and tactics and mobilized other resources (especially money, personnel, and communication networks) necessary for successful social action ...' (quoted in Dym and Hutson, 2005: 75). Black women, Dym and Hutson (2005: 76) go on to observe, 'organized protests through networks, relationships and cooperation ... not through hierarchical positioning'. These women, who played such a constructive and valuable role in working towards gaining civil rights for African-Americans, used their understanding of their subject position as black women to enact leadership within institutional structures with which they were familiar.

The understanding that the women presented here have regarding their experiences of and paths to leadership, similarly illustrate a recognition of their 'outsider' status. Even though they belong to different generations May Blood's reading of the male-dominated power structures within her social and working environment and Sayeeda Khan's belief in the need to build alliances so as 'to avoid being ground down by people who have decided that you are not worth anything. Or that you are to be pigeon-holed' demonstrate awareness of and the need to negotiate the social, cultural and political environments in which they live and work. Their accounts also provide more specific insights into the outcomes that emerge when the women 'do' gender within different sets of institutional structures and processes. In an earlier paper (Elliott and Stead, 2008) we suggested that – paradoxically – it is their position outside traditional power structures that provide them with insights to develop strategies to negotiate their way to their desired role. So, for example, a young Betty Boothroyd's secretarial position allowed her to observe MPs in action and led her to believe she could perform the role of MP as well as anyone else. Nevertheless we can discern differences in how the nine women make sense of their leadership experience. From the way in which May Blood explains the performance of her role as shop steward within a dominant masculine culture for example, we can infer an approach that recognises the need, at some level, to play the men at their own game. Betty Boothroyd's articulation of her path to MP and then Speaker of the House of Commons suggests that she believed she needed to perform the role better than male MPs. She needed to demonstrate her resilience and determination – her 'grit' and 'north country attitude' to follow her chosen path. Tanni Grey-Thompson and Sayeeda Khan in contrast, attribute more explicitly the role of personal networks – family and friends – when articulating their path.

What the women leaders' accounts of their experience within particular institutional and social structures imply is that despite the volume of texts on leadership, leadership still tends to be written about in rather restricted ways. While our study is modest in size our hope is that its critical, in-depth approach illuminates leadership as something that is not necessarily about individuals' career moves, or a role that can only be performed by a small number of individuals within identifiable organisational structures. Sinclair and Wilson (2002) propose that future forms of leadership will need to be more open to difference and more flexible. They argue that the 'tough guy' template of leadership that values the 'solitary and self-reliant hero' (p. 115) is increasingly inappropriate in business contexts that are more demographically diverse and that operate extensively across national and cultural boundaries. In such contexts what is needed are not leaders who are just familiar with local and international business practices. Rather, they suggest, this greater diversity of contexts 'requires diplomats' who are 'willing and able to appreciate how business intermeshes with broader social and cultural practices' (p. 111), individuals who are not company men [*sic*] who have spent much of their career in one organisation. Continuing to appoint leaders who are members of 'a closed or insular élite' (ibid.), chosen because they have attended élite business schools or universities runs the risk of reinforcing and rewarding a narrow form of leadership that tends to 'neglect systemic and structural sources of disadvantage' investing its hopes in 'free markets and open competition as the means to remove inequities' (p. 121).

While Sinclair and Wilson's proposals build on their research with 30 Australian business leaders and so differs in its empirical setting from our own study, other aspects of their methodology are similar. They adopted a discursive narrative approach to their interviews to explore leaders' childhoods and early experiences in order to understand whether these experiences impacted upon their leadership practice. Unlike our own interviewees however, who in their accounts demonstrate the ability to understand and negotiate gendered discourses in a variety of contexts and who recognise the significance of their upbringing and early experiences in forming their practice, Sinclair and Wilson's interviewees by contrast viewed their background as irrelevant to their approach to leadership. This may be, Sinclair and Wilson (2002) suggest, because they must 'learn how to 'pass' as a fully paid up member of the dominant group' (p. 75). Possibly because they do not work in corporate settings, what we have learned from the women we have profiled is that operating outside institutional structures encourages an approach to leadership that can 'hear and recognise the validity of different ways of looking at and experiencing the world' and that has the 'courage to stand up to the status quo, and argue for and practice a different way of doing things' (Sinclair and Wilson, 2002: 112).

Exploring women leaders' accounts leads us to a different understanding of leadership that has inevitable consequences for leadership learning and development, which we explore in the following chapter.

Concluding thoughts

This chapter has drawn together discussions in earlier chapters to consider the implications for women's leadership identity arising from the relationship between dominant institutional gender discourses and social discourses more broadly. We argued that if we are to develop a deeper understanding of the dominance of the 'tough guy' template (Sinclair and Wilson, 2002) of leadership identity then it's necessary to pay closer attention to societal narratives of gender, and the relationship between discourse and the material world. This includes the way these narratives are mobilised within outlets such as the mainstream media and popular culture, in addition to organisation-based gender discourses. We examined how women leaders' awareness of dominant gender discourses and associated power relationships provided them with the opportunity to perform certain leadership identities that worked to disrupt dominant discourses. In observing how the women leaders disrupt dominant discourses, our analysis has led to a conceptualisation of leadership that draws attention to it as a relational process. From this perspective we view leadership as a process through which leaders, followers and other significant stakeholders influence interpretation of their particular setting through discursive actions and practice (Grint, 2000; Kempster, 2009).

In the final section of the chapter we suggest how greater appreciation of individuals' understanding of discourses reveals ways in which institutional structures and processes can be shifted. Developing an understanding of how women learn to negotiate discourse in order to perform new forms of leadership identity helps form the approach to leadership development that we propose in the following chapter.

Notes

1. Critical approaches to the study of organisation arose from the linguistic turn in philosophy and social theory (Rorty, 1967). Within the context of organisation studies this approach takes 'human communication not simply as one element of organizational life, but as *the* essential process – that which calls into organization into being, crafting actuality from possibility' (Ashcraft and Mumby, 2004: xviii). Communication is therefore understood as not only expressing but also producing, organizational realities.
2. In *The Associate* the character of Laurel Ayres, played by Whoopi Goldberg, realises that if she is to have a successful career on Wall Street she either has to work for an older white man or be a white male. She therefore invents an elusive character, Robert Cutty, in order to establish an investment firm.
3. *North Country* is a dramatisation of a group of female Minnesotan mine workers – who become the first women to work at the Eveleth mines – legal battle with their employers was launched due to the hostile environment in which they found themselves working.

6
Women Learning Leadership

> I went to the transport and general union – they afforded me any education I had I have to say. And at times it was difficult. I found myself as the only woman in a whole room full of men but I learned a lot from that experience. Just sitting there quietly listening. ... An example I always give is for instance – I remember being in a room full of men and they were arguing about the world cup and that their firm would not allow them to watch the match live. The day before I went to that I was asking my employer for toilet rolls. And that taught me that women were not asking for nearly enough. We were just taking whatever was given. ... And so I began to use the union more or less as a platform.
>
> —Baroness May Blood, community activist

This quote from May Blood, of her time working in a linen mill and as a union representative, exemplifies the focus of this chapter; how women learn leadership. In particular it indicates the significance of learning as being informal and emerging from the doing of leadership and we explore this in more detail later. The quote also points to the significance of gender, how she was often the only woman, and how women were not asking for enough. Through women leaders' accounts Chapter 4's analysis illustrated how gender is reproduced through social interaction and through organisational processes. This analysis demonstrated that women have to negotiate gendered processes in order to achieve and maintain leadership roles. Furthermore, it foregrounded that women leaders had limited learning opportunities from social networks to help them do this.

Chapter 5 then discussed the implications of our examination of women's experiences for women's leadership identity. In particular this chapter examined why women are not readily identified as leaders. It did this through Ashcraft and Mumby's (2004) framework that draws together different approaches to understanding the relationship between discourse, gender and organisation. By considering identity as a 'discursive product or effect' (Ashcraft and Mumby, 2004: 18), the chapter concluded that women's leadership identity can be shifted when individuals learn to negotiate gender discourses inherent to many institutional structures and processes.

These analyses in Chapters 4 and 5 then raise important questions for women's learning of leadership. These include, how do women leaders learn to negotiate gendered processes and dominant notions of leadership identity? How then does exploring this learning inform leadership development for women? We address these questions in this chapter in four parts. First, we introduce an understanding of the learning of leadership as both formal and informal, and as a socially situated practice. This understanding of learning has resonance with our view of leadership as relational, as outlined earlier in Chapter 3. Here we also draw attention to how such an understanding of learning alerts us to considerations of power relations, that is, access to and control over resources that enable learning (Contu and Wilmott, 2003; Lave and Wenger, 1991). Second, we discuss the relationship between gender, leadership learning and leadership development with a particular focus on learning itself as a gendered process. Third, we introduce our discussion of the ways in which women leaders are learning to negotiate decision-making processes and practices in their work. Here we focus on the ability of women to recognise the impact of gender on their leadership role and the ability of women to 'story' themselves as leaders (Gherardi and Poggio, 2007). Finally, our fourth section proposes ideas for a development workshop for women leaders framed by the Leadership Web that we introduced in Chapter 2 and that draws on ideas of learning as a social and situated practice.

Learning leadership

In our exploration of women's accounts of leadership in Chapters 3 and 4 we observe that women learn ways to advance their careers as leaders through their practice of leadership, for example, through developing supportive female networks. This highlights that learning leadership can be seen as informal as well as formal, such as classroom-based learning. Studying the ways in which individuals informally learn leadership, whether this be in order to 'pass' as a leader, or in learning to become adept at negotiating institutional structures in order to effect change, has been relatively neglected. An important exception to this is a study of leadership learning through lived experience conducted by Kempster (2006). In his study he notes that formal development interventions had a relatively low level of influence on the directors he interviewed whereas there was a marked prominence of learning through the observation of others. However, as Kempster points out, his study is based on interviews with men and he notes that there remains a gap in research into women's learning of leadership through lived experience. We aim to begin to address this gap in this chapter.

A more socially situated approach to understanding leadership considers leadership as a relational concept (Raelin, 2003). Here the leader is not an individual who sits apart from the social context where they are working. This in turn encourages a socially situated approach to learning. For instance, Stead's (2005) study of mentoring finance directors in the National Health Service observes that mentoring as an experience-based activity is as much a relationship between individual and organisation as a relationship between individuals. Then, understanding how women leaders experience learning from a situated approach, is to recognise that any woman leader's experience cannot be separated from its social context. A situated learning perspective, according to Hamilton (2006b: 7) 'views learning as embedded within and as an inextricable part of everyday social practice'. Taking note of the way individuals learn leadership in a variety of social and geographical settings is one step towards not only broadening understandings of leadership, but also in providing a basis for reconceiving how we understand and practice leadership development. For example, Rebecca Stephen's leadership is variously located in different geographical locations and this means that in order for her to develop as a leader she will need to gain an understanding of the social and physical limitations of such locations. Kempster's (2006) research argues that leadership learning reflects processes of situated learning. He writes 'leadership learning through lived experience draws on a complex milieu of events and influences that occur through daily engagement within particular contexts, and it is through such engagement that leadership meanings, practices and identities are developed'. (ibid.: 5).

Learning leadership is acknowledged here as an informal and socially situated practice. Learning as a social and situated practice acknowledges that 'learning takes place as we participate in social practice in a particular, historical and social context (Hamilton, 2006b: 9). Lave and Wenger (1991) for example, suggest that learning is not just a formal, explicit activity but is essentially a social process that is part of, or bounded to, a particular activity. An evaluation study by Stead (2004), for instance, observes that learning emerges from routine everyday work tasks. Drawing on Ellström (2001), she notes how such learning becomes 'formalized' through developmental interventions such as the use of reflective processes. Hamilton (2006a) provides a vivid illustration of learning as a social process when presenting her work on entrepreneurial families. She shows how the learning of family business is embedded in the everyday practice of the family, and so passed down through the generations simply by the presence of individual family members around the business from a very young age. Children for example, begin to learn about the business by going out with a parent as they make customer deliveries.

Following Hamilton this then suggests a focus in the learning of leadership on understanding the dynamics of social interaction and relationships that leaders are engaged with. This has resonance with our understanding from our study of women leaders' experiences that leadership is relational. By relational, as we explored in Chapters 3 and 4, we mean that experiences are what Morrell and Hartley refer to as 'relationally configured' (2006), that is, they are given meaning by relationships with others and the social environment.

A focus on the dynamics of social interaction and leaders' relationships necessarily draw attention to power relations. Referring to Lave and Wenger's work (1991), Contu and Wilmott (2003: 285) note that a situated learning perspective aims to embrace considerations of power with reference to how resources are organised and controlled within particular 'communities of practice'. Leadership might be seen as a community of practice, that is, 'a particular set of relations between people and social activity in the world, over time, which makes up a particular community' (Hamilton, 2006b: 11). Communities of practice share knowledge and become what Contu and Wilmott (2003: 284) describe as 'locales' of learning.

Learning emerging from communities of practice can therefore be hindered or eased by the way in which resources are accessed or organised. For example, in our study of women leaders, we observed in Chapter 4 how women can be excluded from professional networks either through lack of comfort within networks, through a focus on particular social activities that are traditionally masculine such as golf or through not being seen as having the legitimacy to join such networks. Viewing leadership learning as socially situated invites us to consider how such networks are socially produced including the power relations that enable or block access to important learning processes such as professional networks.

If leadership learning is an informal and socially situated practice, leadership development might then be seen less as the development of a single person (leader development), but rather as the development of the practice of leadership (leadership development) (Iles and Preece, 2006). Dym and Hutson (2005) describe leadership development as:

> the unfolding of a system; less as a pattern strictly defined by following, and more as a mobilization of organizational or community resources to achieve collective ends.
>
> (p. 10)

If we recognise the learning of leadership as informal and socially situated, we are necessarily concerned to move beyond models of leadership development that focus on the individual. This view of learning encourages us to identify forms of leadership development that are based on the informal, that is, how women and men experience leadership in their daily practice, and that pay attention to the social conditions and relationships that shape that experience.

Gender and leadership learning

Through our own and others' research, our view of leadership learning has come to be informed by the view that leadership experiences occur within, and are given form by, concrete social conditions, whether this be through being a working-class woman or a black female barrister. When we then explore leadership development we recognise that an individual's experience of leadership development is not therefore only confined to what Brah and Hoy term 'the experience of the subject' per se, but is also focused 'on the struggles around the way that experience is interpreted and defined and by whom' (1989: 72). Brah and Hoy define such struggles as being 'constructed around relations of power between different social groups around cleavages such as racism, class, gender, and sexuality' (1989: 72). Citing Brah and Hoy, Swan (2007: 204) observes, 'all experience is shaped by concrete social conditions, for example being black or white working class, and the significance and making sense of this experience is determined by how and by whom it is interpreted'. The centrality of these struggles then suggests leadership development as a process that enables participants to examine and interpret their experience of leadership through analytical frameworks based on fundamental organising practices such as gender (Brah and Hoy, 1989). Thus in relation to our data, by exploring women leaders' experience through a gender lens, we can, for example, begin to explore how being a woman impacts upon their role as a leader within their particular organisation. We shall explore later in this chapter in more detail the implications of acknowledging gender as fundamental to how we, as leadership developers, might then develop women leaders.

Before we do that however, we believe it is important to examine some of the assumptions upon which theories of learning are built, specifically their lack of attention to gender.

Understanding learning as a gendered process

Within the area of management and leadership development in recent years there has been an increasing acceptance as discussed above that learning is something which is 'social' (ref. to Swan, 2006b). However, what is seen to constitute the social often remains undefined. Nevertheless there is a growing understanding that learning is a process that is relational, situated and socially reproduced. Developing Swan's earlier work on what constitutes the social (2006b), Swan et al., (2009) argue that the 'social' in social learning approaches is rarely conceived as something structured and defined by either gender, race or class. Consequently, the social is presented as an atemporal, ungendered, apolitical, free-floating context of relations (Fenwick, 2005; Hughes, Jewson and Unwin, 2007; Swan et al., 2009).

As we note in our work with Swan (ibid.), while social understandings of learning conceptualise learning as dynamic and relational, what is taken to be the 'social' is rendered curiously static and one-dimensional. This implies the social as a phenomenon constructed 'just there', that floats freely outside the cultural, the public, the historical, the economic, the geographic and the political (Hughes, Jewson and Unwin, 2007).

In feminist theory more broadly however, the 'social' and its relation to gender is much discussed (Swan et al., 2009). Furthermore, how the social is being reconfigured with changing gendered relations is also theorised. Hence, the social is not simply understood as static but is conceptualised as something that is structured by gendered relations and being reshaped by the changing nature of these relations. The women leaders' experiences of gendered processes that we explore in Chapter 4 provides a useful illustration. For example, May Blood's experience of few women being involved at senior levels in local party politics led her to form a party with other women leaders that would focus on women's and children's concerns. In this way, the social condition of being a woman in party politics and not having influence was reshaped by developing a new party where the social condition of being a woman in party politics had influence. This account might be interpreted as an example of how May Blood entered the masculine public arena of political action using the non-threatening issues of women and children. Thus, by adhering to the domestic and hitherto private domain of women and children her party is not interfering with or attempting to influence the publicly political agenda. This focus on the domestic and the private brings a new focus and thus provides her and her colleagues with legitimate access to senior decision-making levels. This example can then be viewed as an instance of redefining what is seen to be political and thus expanding our understanding of the social.

In relation to the situated learning approach more specifically, and in particular when looking at learning from experience, there has been little debate on the gendered aspects of learning relationships (Salminen-Karlsson, 2006). And yet, as we note, particularly in our discussion of gender in Chapter 4 there is much literature on gender in organisations including examinations of how gender is 'done' within organisations (West and Zimmerman, 1987), and an acknowledged understanding in both organisation and management studies that organisational practices co-create gender (Ashcraft and Mumby, 2004). Salminen-Karlsson (2006) contends that, debates of 'doing gender' and debates of situated learning share a view that 'see interaction and practice in various forms as key concepts in the formation of identity' (p. 32). Thus, gender and situated learning debates illuminate the significance of social interaction and the experiences emerging from leadership practice as significant to development.

This has resonance with our findings from our exploration of data in Chapters 3 and 4. In particular it chimes with our finding that women leaders' experiences provide an interpretation of leadership as a social and dynamic network of practice that is impacted significantly by gender. Our discussion in Chapter 4 for example, uses Wharton's (2005) understanding of gender as embedded in social processes to highlight the ways in which it functions as a fundamental organising practice. This analysis reveals the significance of gendered practice for women leaders and for their development. For instance, our focus on gender draws attention to widespread views that variously position women as either without ambition or as suited to a restricted range of organisational functions and roles.

If, as we elaborate in our discussion of gender in Chapter 4, leadership is shaped by fundamental organising practices such as gender, and if we acknowledge that learning results from experiences of practice, then we must recognise that gender will shape our learning of leadership and consequently how we might develop leaders.

Towards the development of women leaders

Our discussions of gender observe that a number of empirical studies of leadership present ways in which men are regularly seen as 'the "natural" inhabitants of organizational life' while women remain 'out of place' (Ford, 2006: 81). Given this, alongside the way in which gender is largely ignored in examinations of the social in social learning theory, it is perhaps not surprising that these understandings are also reflected in leadership development and its practice. As we observe in our exploration of leadership development in Chapter 1, many formal leadership development programmes contribute to understandings of leadership as male through the use for example, of military metaphors (Gabriel, 2005). Furthermore, Roan and Rooney (2006) in their study of work-based learning note that while ideas of situated and social learning may offer insights into how people become practitioners, there is little challenging of gender issues and barriers. Organisational practices including the development of leaders consequently continue to be predominantly constructed and regarded as 'gender neutral'.

How then, in our consideration of women's leadership development, might we reflect women's experiences in how we understand and practice women leaders' development?

Taking a view of leadership learning as an informal as well as a formal process (Fox, 1997; Marsick and Watkins, 1997), and understanding that learning is a social process that emerges from engaging in and being involved in the practice of leadership (Hamilton, 2006b; Kempster, 2006), highlights the importance of leaders' experiences in both the learning and development of leadership. In particular it illuminates for us the concrete social conditions of leadership practice, what it is to be a woman leader (Brah and Hoy in Swan, 2007). In seeking to develop women leaders we might then focus on how women learn to lead from their experiences of negotiating the kinds of gendered processes we discuss in Chapter 4. So how might women deal with networks that place a large focus on traditionally male activities such as golf?

Our analysis of women's accounts in Chapter 4, in which we discuss the extent to which gender impacts upon women's leadership, indicates that women leaders encounter significant barriers in their practice of leadership. For example, women's career advancement may be limited with reduced access to role models and mentors, which then equates to less access to opportunities for learning about how they might overcome difficulties and barriers in their careers (Herzfeld et al., 2008). However, it is important to remember that there are women who are advancing their careers and that there are women in senior roles. Women therefore, are finding ways to be leaders in spite of barriers.

The women's accounts articulated in our study and women's experiences drawn from other studies illustrate two particular ways in which they learn how to negotiate leadership, that is, how they can gain access to and involvement in leadership activities such as decision-making. These ways are: the ability to recognise the impact of gender on their position as a woman leader, and the ability to 'story' themselves as leaders. In the following section we discuss each of these in turn with the aim of gaining a better understanding of how women learn leadership. We then explore how such understanding might inform ideas for the development of women leaders.

Recognising the impact of gender

The accounts from our study and the accounts drawn from other studies illustrate an awareness among women leaders of power relationships within their 'communities of practice'. This includes their learning of how organisational and work practices are gendered. May Blood for instance, when recalling her work in a linen mill, talks about how men dominated the managerial workforce and how women were expected to be grateful for being given a job. Sayeeda Khan notes how men were more likely to be offered better positions than women once they had finished their degrees. Jackie Fisher observes how career expectations of girls differ and Tanni Grey Thompson reflects on the differing perceptions of women once they have a family. Rebecca Stephens remarks on a perceived lack of ambition in competing with men on expeditions. Dawn Gibbins raises the issue of old boy networks and how after hours socialising excludes women. Judith Donovan and Rennie Fritchie both give accounts of how women are hindered from gaining entry to management positions and Betty Boothroyd acknowledges the importance of encouraging and supporting women in their role as political leaders. These accounts link to research that has noted the importance of attending to broader social networks and relational practices to gain career advancement (Beer, 1999; Khuruna, 2003).

Each of these examples from women's accounts might be seen as illustrations of what Gherardi and Poggio (2007) label 'relational dynamics'. What they mean by this is the way that power and inter-personal relations intersect. Thus they write that the term 'relational dynamics' refers to the experiences of leadership, and in particular 'the subjective relationship with power and its implications for interpersonal relations' (ibid.: 159). Gherardi and Poggio's 'relational dynamics' is then more focused than our broader concept of rela-tionality as outlined earlier in the introductory chapter and again in Chapter 3. Our use of the idea of relational when talking about leadership is to get at micro and macro levels, to encompass relation-ships with others and also to the organisational and wider social environment. Their more specific definition is helpful here because it alerts us to power relations in particular in relationships with others.

An example from Hartman's work (1999) helps us illustrate how understanding the gendered nature of such relational dynamics can be helpful for women leaders in the learning of leadership. Nafis Sadik, Special Adviser to the United Nations Secretary General is one of the women leaders profiled in Hartman's edited collection of interviews with women leaders (1999). She recalls that as the only woman representative on a United Nations committee, she became aware that as a woman she was always complimented on her appearance. In her interview she says that she interpreted this in part as a tactic by her fellow committee members, a way of trying to 'neutralize' her contributions that would in effect flatter her and therefore prevent her from raising contentious issues. The interview records:

> At first she joked that whereas they might look forward to seeing her saris, they were unlikely to be looking forward to what she had to say. But then she hit on the idea of returning the compliments, with effusive exclamations on the men's suits or ties or comments on their youthful appearance. "I must say I didn't at first do it deliberately, but rather just as a way of saying something nice back to them. But to men, it comes as a great shock when they're complimented on their looks or their clothes, and it doesn't come as a shock to me: I'm quite happy." She adds: "These compliments and joking about how we looked actually helped me in introducing more serious gender perspectives on many issues, including family planning and the rights of women".

This account can be used to illustrate how 'doing gender', that is, acting in a way that is seen to be appropriate to one's gender, is employed as a tactic, as a way of negotiating influence and leadership. While the interviewee recognised the remarks on her appearance as complimentary she also indicates that the men are assuming that because she is a woman such compliments will flatter her and therefore make her less willing to raise confrontational or difficult issues. In this way the men, in using flattery to keep the woman happy, might be seen to be doing gender. Returning the compliments enables Nafis Sadik to alter the norm of only women's appearance being remarked upon, and so to make compliments on clothing commonplace for men too. This then positions her and them on a symbolically more equal footing and makes it more acceptable for her to be complimented and yet simultaneously confrontational.

Our own research provides another example of how an awareness of the impact of gender is used to negotiate leadership. This example focuses less on the relational dynamics between people. Rather it emphasises an awareness of the gendered nature of organisational systems and structures.

May Blood's account of developing a political party so that women might be represented at the Northern Ireland peace talks illustrates an awareness of how systems and structures might privilege particular concerns. A recognition that the main political parties in Northern Ireland in the 1990s failed to offer representation of women's issues provided her, she believed, with the opportunity to help develop a new political party. Her account acknowledges the need to gain representation through the existing system; '... if I wanted to change the system then I had to work inside'.

Her account provides an example of how an awareness of gendered processes can help women leaders understand where they might best be able to influence. May Blood found that in order to influence she needed to find a way to work within the system. Identifying where women might be able to influence can mean focusing on those areas that have lesser status. So, in May Blood's account the representation of women's issues was not seen as significant by other political parties. This then offered a way in for May Blood and her colleagues that was neither a threat nor in competition with other parties' interests.

Similarly, Judith Donovan's account as related in Chapter 3 provides us with a further example of finding ways to influence through focusing on areas that are perceived to be less important. In this account she recalls becoming Chair of Bradford Training and Enterprise Council in the early 1990s.

In her account Judith Donovan highlights that there was a lack of interest among the business community in working with an initial steering group that was later to become the Training and Enterprise Council. She however saw this as an opportunity to gain a decision-making role. Similar to May Blood's account, her account shows an awareness of an opportunity that could lead to a position of influence. We can also interpret here an awareness that this opportunity exists due to its perceived lesser status and, as Judith Donovan goes on to explain later in her interview, a lack of monetary reward. Thus in these accounts the women highlight their learning of how to find ways to influence through identifying opportunities that due to their lesser status are within their grasp.

Women 'storying' themselves as leaders

Aligned to developing an awareness of the impact of gender and in particular how gender is reproduced through organisational practices, the women's accounts also illustrate the importance of learning how to imagine and present oneself as a leader. Women can find it difficult to envisage or label themselves as leaders. For example, one of our interviewees May Blood said she hadn't thought of herself as a leader. Another one of our interviewees, Jackie Fisher, observed that young women often tend to have more limited career aspirations than young men. This difficulty to envisage oneself as a leader might be attributed to a range of factors including women having fewer role models, there being fewer women in senior positions and as discussed earlier, women having limited access to influential social networks. Storying oneself as a leader, that is, imagining and presenting oneself as a leader, however is an important leadership ability according to current research (Gherardi and Poggio, 2007; Shamir et al., 2005). Gherardi and Poggio (2007: 162) for example, in their work on a 'reflexive' leadership workshop for women managers write that 'storytelling provides not only the opportunity to discuss things that happened or could happen', but also, they write, it offers the opportunity of 'performing one's identity as power holding in situated circumstances'. In other words the ability to narrate one's experiences as a leader, they contend, offers the chance to present oneself as a leader and as someone with authority and influence. Indeed Parry and Hansen (2007: 290) go so far as to say that 'if women cannot be storied as leaders, they cannot be leaders'. In similar vein, Ford et al. (2008: 116) note that use of the words 'leader' and 'leadership' is instrumental in their very construction 'in that they provide an identity, or a way of being, a self, for the people charged with the tasks of leadership'. Furthermore being able to present experiences and accounts of being in a leadership role enables reflection upon one's understanding of leadership (Shamir et al., 2005). Thus women learning to identify themselves as leaders and recounting their experiences as leadership experiences might be seen as significant steps not only in women positioning themselves as leaders but also in analysing and developing understanding about the power relations in their practice of leadership. The storying of leadership could then take on particular significance as a social learning activity, that is, a way to enable women to share experiences and to make their learning and knowledge of leadership explicit.

An account provided by Rennie Fritchie when we were gathering our data is helpful in exploring the importance of storying oneself as a leader as a way of gaining influence. During her interview with us Rennie Fritchie talks about her experience of women introducing ideas at meetings that are then ignored only for these ideas then to be picked up later by men, who then gain credit for the ideas. She explains how she deals with this kind of situation:

> I also find that women when they do it [raise an idea] may not be heard and then later on a man says the same thing and everyone says oh what a brilliant idea ... and I have now learned a tactical tool, so I will say, 'can I just say thank you that was really great and you certainly have taken this to the next stage. I wonder if we can go back to Sally because she suggested this direction a few moments ago and she may have more to say about it than she had at the time.' So I am going to get Sally not just her recognition but her possibility of ownership and adding to it, and therefore I think we have to find ways of doing that and becoming skilled at that.

In this example Rennie Fritchie gives her interpretation of how she deals with a particular type of situation. She highlights that when a woman puts forward an idea it may be overlooked, but when a man then presents the same idea he is more likely to be acknowledged and therefore the idea is recognised as his idea. This privileging of one idea over another has the effect of negating the woman's ownership of the idea. By identifying the idea as belonging to Sally, Rennie Fritchie might be seen to be effectively role-modelling ownership of an idea. Connecting the idea to the person who originated the idea, enables the individual concerned to develop it further. Taking ownership publicly then has the effect of storying her as a leader. The storying of leadership is made explicit within the social setting of a meeting and reinforces the woman's identity as leader.

Vinnicombe and Bank's (2003: 187) interviews with Veuve Clicquot award winners provide a further example of storying oneself as a leader through their profile of Debbie Moore, founder of Pineapple Brand fashion wear and the Pineapple Dance Studio in London's Covent Garden. They note:

> Her office is decorated with photos of her achievements, a half dozen awards, including the Veuve Clicquot Business Woman of the Year Award, displayed prominently, pictures of herself and former prime minister John Major, another photo of her with Lady Thatcher, a few photos of her from her modelling days.

This excerpt describes how Debbie Moore uses images such as photographs and awards to make her leadership visible. Gatrell and Swan (2008) observe that gendered processes are also manifest in the language and symbols of organisations, for example, in the way in which leaders and leadership might be described and in visual images used to denote leaders. The use of images such as photographs and awards can therefore provide a way to present different understandings of leadership and counter what Wajcman refers to as the dominant masculine symbolism of organisations (1998). Displaying these pictures and awards in her office announces Debbie Moore's success as a leader. This excerpt and the account by Rennie Fritchie also highlight that the storying of leadership is a public activity that needs to be shared with others. The sharing of women's experiences and making women's leadership practice public enables us to see how women learn to develop themselves as leaders.

To summarise, this discussion has noted how recognising the impact of gender and storying oneself as a leader are both abilities that women leaders learn to develop in order to negotiate gendered processes. The examples provided here demonstrate deliberate choices made by women in order to gain influence and to be seen as leaders. Indeed, we might argue that as leadership is largely associated with masculinity, women, as outside that norm, therefore have to make conscious decisions on how to work within what Ford et al. (2008) call 'masculinist cultures'. As women are not seen as 'natural' inhabitants of the leadership role, this means learning ways in which they can work within such masculinist cultures in order to present themselves as leaders and to be understood as leaders. With limited access to role models and influential networks women have less opportunity to develop ways of learning to negotiate such cultures and to develop their identity as leaders. Women leaders' accounts are therefore important in that they illuminate examples of how women are learning leadership. These range from identifying opportunities that have little status but offer a way into decision-making, to affirming one's role as a leader through use of visual imagery and by making ownership of ideas publicly explicit. Our interpretation of women leaders' accounts of negotiating gendered processes illustrates learning as a relational process, that is, the product of social conditions, for example, May Blood taking advantage of a lack of interest in women's issues to develop a political party. The accounts of women leaders also provide insight into the gendered aspects of learning relationships which we noted are largely missing in debates and perspectives of experiential learning (Salminen-Karlsson, 2006). For instance, Nafis Sadik's account (Hartman, 1999) of how she employed compliments on her saris to gain a more equitable standing with her male colleagues, shows how her alertness to gendered behaviour enabled her to maintain her leadership role at decision-making talks. Our discussion has also sought to examine the ways in which women leaders develop their leadership identity, that is, how they story and present themselves as leaders. It suggests that by storying themselves as leaders women then role-model their learning for other women. Using gender as an analytical framework through which to explore the accounts of women leaders therefore has significance for both understanding the conditions under which women practice and learn leadership, and for identifying the ways in which women negotiate gendered processes in order to maintain and sustain leadership. So how then might we incorporate this understanding of women's learning leadership into the ways in which we develop women leaders?

In the following sections we aim to address this question by proposing a framework for leadership development. This is based on our analysis of the ways in which leading women are able to identify, interpret and negotiate social practices and processes.

Developing women leaders with *The Leadership Web*

In Chapter 3 we described how we have drawn on our own and others' research to develop what we term a Leadership Web. The Web is intended to illustrate the spheres of influence that our analysis has shown to be significant to women in their becoming leaders, and is intended to convey our understanding of leadership as gendered and relational. In this section we present how the Leadership Web can play a role in facilitating an approach to leadership development that sits within a situated learning framework. The Leadership Web helps to highlight for example, how leadership draws on and connects to the contexts, cultures and activities of the leaders involved. This situated approach, in drawing upon experience, encourages the use of a range of processes to aid leaders to reflect upon, analyse and develop insights into their own leadership practice. The Leadership Web might therefore be used when working with women who are at different stages in their career. For instance, it might be used with women who are aspiring to be leaders, as well as with women who are already in leadership positions. A further example of its use is as a tool to facilitate an individual's understanding of the influences upon their leadership practice. This could involve asking the leader to identify the significant influences in their becoming a leader, or by taking a particular section of the framework to explore how it applies to them in a particular situation. This would then enable the leader to explore, for example, the different types of social networks they belong to and have access to and how they are using those networks to influence. Kempster (2006: 15) in his study of directors that explores the influences shaping leadership notes in his findings a theme of learning occurring in everyday events 'through daily interactions and active participations in acts of both "followership" and leadership'. While he notes that learning occurred in this everyday manner he also observes that this informal learning of leadership wasn't necessarily explicit to his interviewees. The Leadership Web, by offering a focus on the experiences of leaders, can therefore provide a means for making informal learning explicit by bringing different relationships with others and with the organisational and social environment into relief.

It is important to note that by placing the focus on a leader's relationships the Leadership Web seeks to attend to the individual and to the social, that is, to the development of the individual leader within, and in relation to others, to work and to their cultural, political and social context. The Leadership Web describes this by noting significant dynamics of the spheres of influence. For instance, within the sphere of influence termed 'relationship to work', we note the importance for women leaders of developing professional networks and alliances in the workplace. The Leadership Web might therefore be used as a way of identifying the dynamics of relationships that women leaders are engaged with, and how they learn to manage those dynamics in order to maintain their leadership role. So for example, in exploring the relationship to work we might develop our learning about how women develop professional networks and alliances. Asking them to recount their experiences thus enables us to learn from their situated learning, their experience of developing and belonging to networks.

The Leadership Web has emerged from our own research findings, has been informed by other examinations of women's leadership and is underpinned by socially situated learning perspectives. The Leadership Web is, as outlined earlier, based on the understanding that learning of leadership is a social and informal practice arising from the experiences and interactions of the social practice of leadership (Hamilton, 2006b; Fox, 1997). An additional intention for the Web is for it to act either as a tool or a reference point in leadership development interventions, and we now go on to provide an example of how it may be used in practice.

The workshop

The example we draw on to present how The Leadership Web may be employed as a developmental tool comes from one of the author's (Stead, 2009) experiences of running a series of workshops with women in leadership roles in UK public service organisations including the National Health Service and local government. The workshop maintains a focus on each participant as a leader in her current role. Its purpose is to raise participants' awareness of themselves as leaders, the social context in which they operate and the significance of individual and social resources (such as networks and alliances) they draw upon to sustain their role. The workshop could be used in multiple ways, for aspiring women leaders, as a career workshop or as a coaching intervention. In this section we explain the structure and process of the workshop including pedagogical processes that might be used.

Running the workshop

The workshop uses stories as the core process and comprises two input sessions; a group reflection session and four key activities for relating experiences, presenting experiences, analysing experiences and identifying actions. The workshop can be run as a series of three half-day sessions, that is, where participants focus on an initial input session and an activity that involves relating experiences on the first half-day, the second input session, an activity that includes presenting and analysing experiences on the second half-day an activity that involves identifying experiences and final group reflections on the third and final half-day. While we would recommend that each of the activities are addressed within a workshop so that participants have the opportunity to share, present, analyse and commit to action, we also recognise that some of these may be shortened depending on time and purpose. For example, participants may choose to focus on one part of the leadership web and so respond to fewer questions in relating their experiences. The workshop demands a degree of trust in relating experiences and being open to questioning and so we would recommend that this be carried out in small groups, ideally of around 12 participants.

Workshop structure and process

Input session

The workshop begins with a 30-minute introduction to gender and organisational theory. This is important for two main reasons (Stead, 2009). First, because it introduces participants to ideas of how gender shapes our leadership practice through our social interactions and through workplace practices and processes, such as recruitment, selection and promotion. Second, because it illustrates how women have different experiences of leadership than men and why it is useful to share those experiences with other women leaders. Useful sources for this input include ideas outlined in Chapter 4 on gender as a fundamental organising practice, also Swan and Gatrell's research on gender and diversity in management (2008). Introducing ideas of gender then enables the participants to relate to gender as a frame through which to make sense of their experience (Brah and Hoy, 1989).

Key activity 1: Relating experiences

Following the initial input participants undertake the first key activity. Here they are asked to consider individually the stories of their leadership using questions informed by the Leadership Web's three spheres of influence. The questions we use are:

1. What aspects of your relationship with others have been most influential for you in your practice as a leader. For example, was it your relationship to your family, have you been guided by female role models, do you gain knowledge and support from personal networks? Please provide a specific example(s).
2. What role does your relationship to place play in your leadership practice, for example, does the physical geography/political climate/local/organisational culture or historical context of where you operate make a difference to how you practise leadership? Please provide a specific example(s).
3. What role does work play in your understanding and practice of leadership? How do you view your position in the workplace? Have you overcome any barriers in working towards a leadership role? Can you identify workplace networks and alliances that have supported you or continue to be important in your leadership practice? What practices and strategies have you employed, or can you identify, to help you negotiate a leadership role?

Participants spend a minimum of 20 minutes on their own responding to the questions. They then work in pairs to develop their stories further. In each pairing the participants spend approximately 20 minutes on each other's stories (40 minutes in total) checking that they have each provided details and examples. If timing is reduced, participants can work on fewer questions or as mentioned earlier, focus on one particular area.

Input session

When participants have developed their stories the group comes together for a further input session of 30–40 minutes. This session anticipates the analysing of experiences and identifying actions (key activities three and four) and introduces critical reflection as a tool for analysis and provides participants with a framework for questioning. Critical reflection is described by Reynolds as questioning and challenging underlying assumptions (1997). Fook and Gardner in their text on critical reflection (2007) suggest modelling the process, so here facilitators may choose to do this by one facilitator relating an account and a second facilitator then questioning the first. Fook and Gardner (ibid.) also offer a range of different types of questions that can act as a framework for probing and for identifying ways forward.

For example, probing questions include 'how did I influence the situation through; my presence, my actions?', 'what perspectives are missing from my account?', 'what assumptions are implicit in my account?', and action oriented questions include, 'what might I do as an individual that will contribute to broader-level collective changes (with immediate colleagues or in my workplace?)' (ibid.: 76–7). Here participants can be provided with a list of questions they can draw upon to help work with each other in the following activities.

Key activity 2: Presenting experiences

Having developed their stories in the first activity, workshop participants go on to present their stories to the other leaders. The individual woman leader presents her own story within a given time slot (10–15 minutes to present). As this can be a lengthy process we recommend dividing the group into smaller groups of four. As we note above, following Gherardi and Poggio's work (2007), we consider the sharing and telling of each other's leadership stories to be significant because it enables each participant to develop a shared sense of each other's leadership learning. This has the further benefit of providing material to use as a foundation in discussions examining connections, similarities and differences as leaders. The telling is therefore different from the thinking in that it enables the women leaders to make their knowledge and learning explicit, and so to enable a collective learning (Easterby-Smith and Lyles, 2003). Thus for instance, exploring the ways in which women draw on networks might identify different strategies for influencing through groups and alliances that other women might be able to employ.

Key activity 3: Analysing experiences

Having presented their stories to their peers, the women are then invited to reflect critically on their experiences. Reynolds drawing on Hindmarsh (1993: 111) notes a particular focus in critical reflection on "the context and 'its institutionalized relationships of class, gender, race and power'". The input sessions on gender, organisational theory and critical reflection provide the framing for this activity. Using the framework of critically reflective questions provided and staying in groups of four, each woman, following the presentation of her story, is questioned by her other three group members for a further 15–20 minutes. It can also be helpful here for one of the groups to take notes of the questions and responses. This role can be rotated.

This questioning of assumptions behind experience facilitates a deeper analysis of what has been going on with the purpose of revealing why as well as how things happen. Critical reflection then may lead to developing insight into power relations, of how influence is wielded and yielded. If we take the example of trying to gain promotion, having narrated her experience of seeking promotion, the woman leader might then be encouraged to reflect on a number of levels. For instance, to reflect on how promotion is dealt with in her organisation she might be asked a range of questions. What kind of work is most likely to lead to promotion in her organisation? Are some forms of work valued more highly than others? What kind of promotions have occurred recently and how do they fit with organisational values? Where does her work fit with these values? This challenging of experience may then lead to what Reynolds (ibid.: 314) terms 'engaging with individual, organisational or social problems with the aim of changing the conditions which gave rise to them, as well as providing the basis for personal change'. In other words by analysing her experience the woman leader may gain insights at a number of levels. Critically reflecting on her experience may enable her to examine more closely the power relations, that is, the organising and controlling of resources (Contu and Wilmott, 2004) that enable access, for example, to leadership activities that may lead to promotion. This in turn may offer insight into how she might gain access to such resources.

Key activity 4: Identifying actions

The final part of the workshop involves women identifying actions that they might take forward. A critically reflective approach to the analysis of women's experiences encourages a commitment to action. Reynolds (1997: 316) highlights that underlying critical reflections 'are the goals of personal development and of betterment of society'. Thus identifying action is important because it involves the participants making a commitment to do something that impacts them personally but also may seek to impact at an organisational level. Gray's critique of women-only management training observes the importance of what she calls 'forward motion' (1994: 228), that is, finding positive ways to move forward. Contu and Wilmott (2003) citing Lave and Wenger (1991) in their argument regarding the importance of power relations in learning theory note that learning processes are integral to the exercise of power and control. Committing to action might then be seen as a way for participants to embed their learning and to enable women leaders to recognise where and what they can change or influence (Stead, 2009). As part of the workshop participants could, following the presenting and analysing of their experiences, work in pairs or trios (up to 30 minutes per person) to identify actions that may be at an individual or wider level. Working in pairs or trios enables women to question each other about how they will carry out that action specifically, whether it is realistic and when they will do it.

Group reflection

Following the identification of actions, we suggest that the workshop is concluded with small groups of four reflecting on the process for 20 minutes. This is intended to give individuals the opportunity to reflect in a number of ways. These ways include thinking about what has been helpful for them, what they have learned from participating in this process as an individual and with reference to their wider working environment and how they might use the critical reflection process in their own practice. Each small group is invited to summarise their discussion and present this summary to the larger group. We would suggest 10-minute presentations and then a further 10 minutes to discuss any issues arising from each presentation. Fook and Gardner (2007) observe the importance of reflecting on process and learning not only as a closing process but also in enabling groups to identify core themes, particularly if participants are from the same workplace. This then provides, they write, the opportunity for groups to spend further time if required on collective action or to identify themes for further development.

Workshop developments

This kind of workshop can lead into other developmental activities. Other ways in which the Leadership Web and processes from the workshop might be used include as part of coaching sessions, career counselling, career workshops and action learning sets (Stead, 2009). For example, the process of critically reflecting upon experiences might be employed to develop peer group action learning sets. The analysis of stories might be used to focus upon how participants influence and network with a view to career development.

On a workshop with women managers in health service organisations for instance, the participants went on to draw a map of their networks indicating the different ways in which those networks and alliances were supportive including acting as a critical friend in decision-making and acting as a guide in career choices.

A further example highlights how this kind of development can be helpful in enabling women to identify common difficulties at work and to explore the different ways that participants deal with these in their own particular situation. In this example a workshop held with a group of public service women leaders revealed that many of them experienced often being the only woman present at senior decision-making meetings. The women expressed feelings of isolation, of sometimes being the centre of attention or conversely of being ignored. The stories of their experiences revealed a range of coping strategies including sitting beside supportive colleagues during meetings, making a point of commenting early on in the meeting so their presence would be noted and being part of women-only networks where they felt they could talk openly about these kind of experiences with other women.

Eliciting these understandings through the narration of their experiences then enables participants to recognise the significance of particular relationships in their leadership practice, the significance of gender in their leadership and the importance they place on particular resources.

Workshop purposes and assumptions

The workshop outlined above contains a number of purposes that are core to the assumptions upon which the Leadership Web is based. First, it aims to encourage women to recognise the development of their leadership in relation to others, and to encourage reflection on the particular sociocultural and political contexts in which this development has taken place. This accords with a view of leadership as a social and situated practice, one that is 'contextualised in specific relational situations and systems' (Gherardi and Poggio, 2007: 159). Attending to leadership learning as a social and situated practice then enables individuals to examine the specific social environment and the relationships that are important in their leadership practice. This is useful because it enables participants to gain insight into what might be helpful ways of working within particular constraints. One example of this from our study of women leaders is Rennie Fritchie recognising that she would need to develop her promotional prospects in an informal way. Viewing learning as a social and situated practice also enables participants to explore the different power relations, so for example, to reflect on who has influence and in what situations.

The workshop is also informed by work proposing that by relating events and experiences leaders are able to reflect on their own concept of leadership (Shamir et al., 2005; Parry and Hansen, 2007). Articulating their practice to themselves and others provides individuals with an opportunity to consider more closely for example, how they have reached their current position and how they might take this learning forward. Who has provided them with support and what experiences have been significant in fostering learning opportunities? This is helpful for participants in understanding sources of support and influence.

The workshop employs the use of stories as its core process. Here we have drawn inspiration in particular from work by Gherardi and Poggio (2007) which examines the use of stories in experiential learning. Their work provides detailed examples of narrative workshops in management education and recognises both storytelling and listening as core to the developmental process. It is in this interaction of storytelling and listening, they write, that individual identities 'are produced and negotiated and that the meaning of experiences is constructed' (ibid.: 165). This has resonance with our data that points to the significance for women learning leadership of being able to 'story' oneself as a leader. Gherardi and Poggio go on to say that storytelling and listening enables a 'collective processing of common experiences' (p. 165) that in turn enables participants to 'reconsider their positioning in individual, professional, and organizational relations' (2007: 165). Thus through the use of stories the workshop aims to provide women leaders with the opportunity to examine not only how they might see themselves and present themselves as leaders but also to explore where they sit in relation to others. In so doing, this kind of intervention aims to encourage individuals to understand and recognise themselves in relation to power.

Contu and Wilmott (2003: 283) observe that taking a situated learning perspective means recognising 'the embeddedness of learning practices in power relations'. They go on to note that storytelling can bring about learning through the sharing of 'context-sensitive understandings of the world of work and of working selves, as well as tasks performed, *(and how they)* are acquired, shared and elaborated' (ibid.: 284). Therefore, by taking a social and situated approach to learning and through the use of storytelling, participants might begin to identify and gain insight into, for instance, what kind of leadership activities are most highly prized within their workplace, how these activities are managed and delegated and who carries out these activities.

The example workshop is also based on the idea of this being a workshop for women leaders. That is not to say that this kind of workshop could not be used with men and women leaders, rather that we present it here as a workshop for women. Gray (1994) notes in her study of women-only management training that there is a danger in focusing on barriers rather than taking a forward looking view that enables women to 'become agents in their own learning and in their choices at work'. (ibid.: 228). Importantly, Gray writes that women-only management training has largely failed to engage with the political by focusing mainly on facilitating individual women's achievement (1994). However, while acknowledging these concerns we suggest that a women-only workshop may have positive benefits.

As we have noted from our research into women's leadership experiences, women face particular issues as leaders due to their gender and we concur with Gray's view that participants on women-only development activities 'have much to contribute and to gain from engaging and struggling with the personal, political and the theoretical' (1994: 229). In designing a workshop that is based on an understanding of learning as a socially situated practice, we therefore invite consideration of the personal, political and theoretical. For instance, asking women to narrate their experiences focuses attention on the women's interactions and relationships. This not only provides a basis from which women might identify struggles and difficulties but also from which women might gain insight into how such situations unfold (the political), the values that underpin such situations (the theoretical) and how she might deal with them (the personal).

Workshop summary

To summarise, leadership learning designed as a shared experience for women leaders is meaningful in that it enables women to collectively identify and share the ways in which they are developing strategies for negotiating and influencing as leaders. Based on the telling of experience as a process through which to learn about ways of leading, it therefore acknowledges the social and situated nature of learning and leadership. Day (2001: 583) writes about leadership as 'a complex interaction between the designated leader and the social and organizational environment'. Through the sharing of experience this kind of development intervention recognises the interaction between leader and environment. It offers a basis from which to examine that interaction and to identify how women leaders might learn ways to not only sustain their leadership but to develop their leadership further and seek to influence organisational change. The presenting, questioning and analysing of experience also enables participants to discuss 'the personal, political and the theoretical' (Gray, 1994: 229) and thereby gain insights into their particular situation, their relationships with others and their options to influence. Committing to actions encourages women to embed their learning and to take positive action in influencing their particular situation.

Conclusion

In this chapter we have sought to explore how women learn leadership and how this then informs the development of women leaders. In particular, we have argued that learning of leadership and leadership development must take into account the way in which leadership experiences are shaped by concrete social conditions such as gender, race and class. This has resonance, we propose, with a situated approach to learning, one that understands learning as informal and social practice emerging from the day to day participation in leadership activities and one that pays attention to power relations. However our discussion notes that situated learning theories pay little attention to gender. Recognising, as explored in earlier chapters through the experiences of women leaders, that gender as a fundamental organising practice shapes leadership, we argue that gender also shapes the learning of leadership. We go on to examine this in more detail by providing examples of how women leaders' learning emerges from an awareness of the impact of gender and through the 'storying' of themselves as leaders. These examples indicate that while women face barriers in their leadership practice and in becoming leaders, they nonetheless are finding strategies for progression. How then, we ask, does women's learning of leadership inform leadership development? We respond to this by proposing a framework for leadership development based on our representation of leadership, the Leadership Web as presented in Chapter 3. In particular we draw inspiration from Gherardi and Poggio's (2007) use of narrative methodology in management education and the use of critical reflection (Fook and Gardner, 2007; Reynolds, 1997). The proposed workshop outlines a development activity that aims to enable participants to use the resource of their experience as individual women leaders. The women are invited to do this within a framework that encourages collective learning of the social conditions that shape their leadership practice and that encourages a commitment to action.

In conclusion, these discussions of leadership learning and development have demonstrated that women leaders' learning of leadership and their development requirements are neither gender-neutral nor individual activities. Rather their learning and development are bound by their being women and bound by their relations to others and their social environment. As such women's leadership learning and development are interpreted as dynamic and shifting, social concepts calling for development activities that focus on the sharing of concrete experiences with a view to personal and organisational improvement. Attending to learning and development in this way, we argue, offers progression for women leaders by affording them the opportunity to analyse their leadership practice and to identify positive ways of influencing and moving forward.

7
Reflections and Conclusions

Studying women and leadership

In earlier chapters we have articulated the observations and experiences that have been influential in convincing us that a study of women leaders can provide fresh insights into understandings of leadership. These formed a series of questions that guided the development of this book including:

1. Why are women leaders still seen as 'out of place' (West and Zimmerman, 2005)?
2. What is currently being written and said about women leaders?
3. Why does the leadership literature continue to be dominated by representations of the leader as individual (male) hero?
4. How are women leaders being represented?
5. What can we learn about leadership by studying it in alternative settings?
6. How can we further the development of new approaches to leadership?
7. How can we better reflect women's experiences of leadership in the practice of leadership development?

In exploring these questions in the process of writing this book, our intention has been to develop an appreciation of how women leaders negotiate gendered processes and societal narratives. Or, in other words, how women leaders learn to take on a leadership identity. Our hope is therefore that the contents of this book will be of interest to:

- women who are aspiring to leadership, and women leaders who are aiming to progress their careers

- leaders who may be working in a variety of settings and who wish to gain influence in order to effect sustainable change
- researchers who are looking for alternative understandings of approaches to, and processes of, leadership
- learning and development practitioners who wish to engage with experiential learning processes that highlight the social, political and cultural context of leadership practice.

In this chapter we therefore conclude the book by reviewing the contributions to leadership theory, practice and research generated by our enquiry.

What we have learnt about women and leadership

The need for new sources of leadership learning

When beginning this book our principal intentions were to ask critical questions of mainstream and traditional understandings of leadership by inviting women to narrate their leadership experiences. In so doing our aim has been to put forward an alternative conception of leadership and leadership development, one that views leadership as something best understood through qualitative methodologies that seek to illuminate the social processes of leadership within particular contexts. The book's focus has been motivated by our experiences, previous academic work, observations and discussions with women colleagues, friends and relatives over a number of years. These various encounters have elicited a number of responses ranging from almost complete despair when reading public reports detailing women's slow progress in gaining positions of influence (Equal Opportunities Commission, 2007; Equality and Human Rights Commission, 2008), to overwhelming hope when hearing the inspirational stories of the women leaders featured in this book. All of which suggested to us that the relatively neglected area of women's leadership offered rich potential for developing an understanding of more creative and socially sustainable approaches to leadership.

To undertake this study, our approach to investigating women and leadership that we present in this book has taken place in three main ways: (1) through an investigation of current literature (Chapters 1 and 2); (2) through an examination of empirical research

(Chapters 3 and 4) and (3) through an analysis of implications for leadership identity and leadership development (Chapters 5 and 6). In undertaking these tasks we have sought to develop a robust case that offers a framing of leadership that foregrounds alternative routes to the learning and practice of leadership.

Our analysis began in Chapter 1 where we observed the limited empirical base of the leadership literature. It is limited both in terms of its target constituency – the white, western male, as well as its preferred research sites – large, modern, western organisations that seem impervious to external influences. Unsurprisingly, we argued, this has resulted in a body of literature implicitly underpinned by white, western, male values. We nevertheless noted that more relational views of leadership are mounting a challenge to this well-established understanding while simultaneously remaining cautious towards the opportunities for women seemingly offered by some postheroic leadership accounts. In Chapter 2 we examined implications arising from the understanding of leadership as located in the individual (male) by studying how women leaders are visually and metaphorically represented. When women leaders are profiled we discovered that they are often depicted in less than flattering ways. Stereotypical images such as Queen Bee, Iron Lady or Selfless Heroine are often called upon to reinforce their difference to men leaders. The individual male becomes reified as the rightful holder of the leadership mantle while his female counterparts struggle not to injure themselves hitting against glass ceilings or falling off glass cliffs. We do not dispute the challenges facing women leaders who do achieve positions of authority and influence, and the statistics clearly show the dominance of white males in leadership positions. However, these representations provide little in-depth critical understanding of the everyday lives of women leaders including the difficulties faced by them and the successes they achieve. Consequently, leadership and leadership development remain broadly conceptualised. Little reference is paid to gender and the impact and effect this has on the practice and experience of leadership. This tendency in the literature therefore silences the experiences of those who do not fit the ideal leader prototype: the white, western, middle-class male working within the bounded organisational setting. Ironically, the much remarked upon volume of leadership literature is rather poor when it comes to its sources for theoretical development and so our understandings of leadership at best remain partial. There is still, it seems, much work to be done to refresh what we understand by leadership and to highlight the alternative ways in which it can be practised, and is being practised, in many different settings.

Stories of women's leadership experiences

An explicit aim in conducting the research for, and then writing, this book is that it has presented an opportunity and a space to engage with narratives of leadership that are less often heard. What has emerged from this engagement has been an appreciation of the significance of relationships in the women's leadership learning and practice. The Leadership Web in Chapter 3 attempts to represent the interconnections between the three sets of significant relationships showing the dynamic, shifting and overlapping nature of them. The old model of the self-reliant individual leader is immediately challenged when we learn how leading women draw on personal and professional networks and alliances that span their relationships to others, to place and to work. These relationships also shift to accommodate their current role and development. Particularly significant is that the women's accounts are marked by the recognition that being female shapes their relationships in specific ways; the women's leadership practice is therefore defined and shaped by their gender. This has been illustrated in terms of their personal life – whether as a mother or a daughter – and the influence, or conversely lack, of female role models. In social and cultural terms too, being a woman grants them lesser status and leads them not to be taken seriously. This also shapes their leadership practice. In the workplace, having to deal with explicit and implicit barriers and often being isolated and excluded, all play a significant role in how they negotiate their leadership practice.

Claiming that a leader's gender influences their practice and identity indicates the need to place leadership within a broader systemic context. While on the one hand we spend time focussing on individuals' narratives, on the other we recognise that leadership can only be made sense of by considering its social, political and cultural context. While this might not seem such a radical approach in other discipline areas, the annexation of the leadership terrain by the management studies literature has witnessed a trend towards psychologically based quantitative studies (Sinclair and Wilson, 2002). The methodologies used in these studies favour breadth over depth and so cannot even begin to reveal the 'how' and why' of leadership that Conger (1998: 109) argues need to be considered if we are going to understand leadership's 'deeper structures'. A claim we make for this book is that it contributes to understanding the how and why of leadership by listening to the ways in which individuals learn and practise leadership, which leads to a greater appreciation of leadership's situated development.

Gender organises leadership

Taking a qualitative approach to this study has highlighted that gender is a fundamental organising practice that works at many levels. As we noted in Chapter 4 how decisions are made and who is promoted, to name just two organisational processes, are gendered. Dominant organisational discourses articulate and reinforce what are deemed to be appropriate leadership behaviours and identities. For example, expectations of what women might achieve are framed by processes that filter women into particular occupations. These processes in turn are mobilised by broader societal narratives on how women perform their identity at work. Analysing women leaders' accounts has highlighted that doing gender cannot be separated from doing power and doing leadership. We recognise the pervasive nature of these narratives including how they are mobilised in popular culture and the media. Film texts for example, can reinforce the construction of women leaders as out of place in work settings (Bell, 2008). Analyses of corporate financial reports also underline feminist research that identifies a gendered division of labour (Benschop and Meihuizen, 2002). We can therefore reach a deeper understanding of how women leaders are marginalised when we are aware of the variety of ways in which narratives of women leaders as different, or as outsiders, infiltrates the material organisational space.

Greater awareness of the significance of gender to leadership helps the development of a more nuanced understanding of why leadership is practised, performed, organised and conceptualised in certain ways. Our approach to this study has shed further light on the reasons for the continued dominance of white males in leadership positions while simultaneously illustrating how women perform gender manoeuvres to interrupt dominant narratives.

Women learning leadership

Accounts of leadership that illustrate the ways in which women become adept at negotiating institutional structures and practices to gain influence, offer creative opportunities for leadership development. As stated in this chapter's introduction, one of our hopes for this book is that it will contribute to the relatively small body of literature concerned with the qualitative examination of leadership learning. Kempster's (2006, 2009) study of how leadership is learnt is an exception to this. He notes the disquiet around the efficacy, or otherwise, of formal leadership development interventions. By contrast, his study argues that informal development in the form of an individual's 'lived experience' is more significant and dominant in accounts of leadership learning. Our study bears comparison to Kempster's in its methodological approach, overall purpose and observations regarding the significance of the situated nature of learning. However, Kempster's main research focus is the experience of men leaders, and he points out the need for further research that attends to women's experiences. Our study therefore differs and extends this work in its focus on women leaders and its exploration of leaders from a range of different settings. Furthermore, in our work the analytic focus of gender as an organising element in leadership learning forces critical questions about the nature of the social that is embedded in social approaches to learning. As we note in Chapter 6 and elsewhere (Swan, Stead and Elliott, 2009) the 'social' in social learning approaches such as experiential and situated learning, is generally presented as an atemporal, ungendered, apolitical set of relations that is free of class and race. Given the number of studies that take for granted men's dominance of organisational spaces and leadership positions, alongside the ungendered way in which the 'social' in social learning theory is regarded, it is easy to understand why leadership development and its practice are often rooted in masculine principles of obedience (Gabriel, 2005). This has inevitable implications for women's leadership development. If women's career advancement is limited because of a lack of access to networks of power, role models and mentors, then in the majority of cases participating in formal leadership development programmes is unlikely to assist women's career progression. Nevertheless there are women who are achieving positions of influence and authority. It is by gaining a more in-depth awareness of their everyday learning of leadership practice that offers us greater potential for alternative development interventions.

Implications for practice: A proposal for women's leadership development

The book culminates in a proposed leadership development intervention that is informed by our study's methodological approach, findings and analysis. In developing the intervention we have been particularly influenced by the process of conducting the research. Listening carefully to women leaders' accounts alerted us to the significance of narrative in structuring organisational practices, as well as the ways in which these narratives can be creatively and productively interrupted. Coupled with an awareness of the sociocultural and political contexts in which leadership and leadership development occur, we propose an intervention underpinned by the view that leadership learning is a social and situated practice.

Employing the use of stories as its core process, the workshop methodology builds on previous work that suggests that relating their experiences offers leaders the opportunity to reflect on their view of leadership (Shamir et al., 2005; Parry and Hansen, 2007). Gherardi and Poggio (2007) provide a detailed illustration of how a narrative methodology can be used in management education workshops. Allowing women the opportunity to story themselves as leaders in the presence of others, provides, we argue, a space in which they can present themselves, and be seen by others, as leaders. The workshop therefore builds on our data which alerts us to the influence that can be accrued by interrupting dominant organisational narratives.

We recognise that proposing a development intervention aimed exclusively at women can be interpreted as contradicting our previous discussions on the relationship between gender, leadership and power. We agree with Gray (1994) that women-only development interventions run the risk of focussing on barriers rather than looking forward. Another weakness is that they are not alert to the political consequences of women-only development as a phenomenon, that is, as a set of interventions that tend to focus on facilitating *individual* women's achievement. A strength we identify for our proposed intervention is that encouraging an awareness of leadership's social, political and cultural context, and reflecting that understanding in the choice of processes that comprise the workshop methodology, gives participants the opportunity to gain insight into the ways in which the relationship between gender, power and leadership unfold. Developing this critical insight offers participants the opportunity to identify and commit to realistic actions that acknowledge their agency and how this can most effectively be mobilised within their specific context.

Implications for theory and practice: The relationality of leadership

Working from a methodological perspective that interprets leadership as a social process, and engaging with accounts of leadership experiences within alternative settings, have drawn attention to the relational aspects of leadership. We have drawn on a number of understandings of the relational including examples in the leadership literature, in developing our conception of leadership and leadership development.

At the empirical level, in analysing the women leaders' accounts of their experience, our attention was drawn to the different sets of relationships that women draw on to develop their leadership practice. Studying women's relationships to others, to place and to work illustrates how leadership is constituted (Grint, 2000), that is, how what leadership is, is interpreted by a range of stakeholders and is influenced by their context and specific situation.

At the theoretical level the frameworks (e.g. Wharton, 2005; Ashcraft and Mumby, 2004) we have drawn on have highlighted the ways in which gender operates at both the micro and macro levels and how these interact with each other. At the micro level, the relational nature of leadership occurs in the ways in which individuals interact with each other including others' perceptions and expectations of women leaders. At the macro level, we note the opaque nature of gendered organisational processes, which build upon unquestioning assumptions of leadership identity as male. By taking a view of leadership identity as shaped through discourse, our attention is drawn to the relationship between discourse, gender, power and organisation. In sharpening our analytical gaze, we develop an appreciation of how women leaders understand, interpret and interrupt this set of discursive and material relationships.

At the practical level, Gherardi and Poggio's (2007) notion of relational dynamics informs the leadership development intervention we propose in Chapter 6. This recognises leadership as a process that involves individuals relating to others within a set of power relationships. In providing illustrations of women's leadership practice, Hartman (1999) discusses how understanding the gendered nature of such relational dynamics can be helpful for women leaders in the learning of leadership. Our research also provides examples that draw attention to women leaders' awareness of the impact of gender and how they use this to negotiate leadership. In the case of the examples we present in Chapter 6 including May Blood's account of the development of a Northern Irish political party, we are made aware of the gendered nature of organisational systems and structures. These examples reveal how an awareness of gendered processes can help women leaders understand where they might best be able to influence.

Viewing leadership as relational requires that we pay attention to: how we undertake research, the relationship between the micro and macro practices that shape leadership and individuals' strategies for learning leadership.

Suggestions for further research

In drawing together the learning gained in the process of conducting this study by proposing a leadership development intervention, we aim to communicate our hopes for the 'forward motion' (Gray, 1994) of women leaders. Nevertheless we suggest that further research is required to deepen our understanding of alternative leadership approaches to inform future development interventions. These might include:

- *Developing leadership's empirical base:* Our research is distinctive in that it makes visible leadership experiences that occur in alternative settings. However, more qualitative research is needed to broaden both the range of settings in which leadership is studied as well as the practices of leaders who do not conform to traditional leader archetypes.

- *Developing methodologies:* We deliberately adopted a narrative approach to this study to ensure that it presented data that was rich enough to analyse the relationship between gender, power and leadership. In addition to conducting research in alternative settings, further research is also needed that pays attention to the relationship of leaders to their social environment.
- *Acknowledging diversity:* It is not only women who are poorly represented in positions of influence. There is also a notable lack of representation from other social groups. Our study mainly focuses on the UK context, but examples we draw on to develop our arguments indicate that the experiences of women in the US for example, point to similar patterns of gendered processes. We also read little about the experiences of black and minority ethnic British women and men leaders, or how those who are considered to be physically disabled learn to negotiate dominant discourses of leadership in order to manoeuvre their way to leadership positions.

Final reflections on researching women's leadership

We hope that our engagement with the experiences of women leaders contributes to the developing body of critical work in leadership studies that is seeking to draw attention to the limitations of dominant perspectives. By profiling leadership experiences that occur in alternative settings, we are arguing that leadership is already being practised in alternative ways. As researchers our intention is to continue to make sense of leadership from a position that recognises the value in attending to its social and cultural roots, that views leadership as a relational process and that moves away from leader-centric perspectives. We hope therefore that this book will encourage the development of further critical research on women's leadership to provide a more inclusive understanding of the breadth and diversity of leadership practice.

References

Abramson, J. (1975) *The Invincible Woman: Discrimination in the Academic Profession*. London: Josey-Bass.

Acker, J. (1990) 'Hierarchies, Jobs, Bodies: A Theory of Gendered Organizations', *Gender and Society*, vol. 4: 139–58.

—— (1992) 'From Sex Roles to Gendered Institutions', *Contemporary Sociology*, vol. 21(5): 565–9.

—— (1995) 'Feminist Goals and Organizing Processes' in *Feminist Organizations: Harvest of the New Women's Movement*, M. M. Ferree and P. Y. Martin (eds). Philadelphia: Temple University Press.

—— (1998) *The Future of Gender and Organizations: Connections and Boundaries*. MA: Blackwell Publishing.

Adair J. (1989) *Great Leaders*. Guildford, Surrey: Talbot Adair Press.

Adler, N. (1999) 'Global Leaders: Women of Influence', in G. Powell (ed.), *Handbook of Gender and Work*. Thousand Oaks, CA: Sage.

Alimo-Metcalfe, B. and Alban-Metcalfe, J. (2001) 'The Construction of a New Transformational Leadership Questionnaire', *Journal of Occupational and Organizational Psychology*, vol. 79: 1–27.

—— (2005) 'Leadership: Time for a New Direction?', *Leadership*, vol. 1(1): 51–71.

Alimo-Metcalfe, B. and Lawler, J. (2001) 'Leadership Development in UK Companies at the Beginning of the Twenty-fsirst Century: Lessons for the NHS?', *Journal of Management in Medicine*, vol. 15: 387–404.

Alimo-Metcalfe, B., Ford J., Harding, N. and Lawler, J. (2001) 'British Companies at the Beginning of the 21st Century: Factors that Impede Leadership Development Initiatives. London: Careers Research Forum.

Alvesson, M. (1996) 'Leadership Studies: From Procedure and Abstraction to Reflexivity and Situation', *The Leadership Quarterly*, vol. 11(4), 581–613.

Alvesson, M., Ashcraft, K. L. and Thomas, R. (2008) 'Identity Matters: Reflections on the Construction of Identity Scholarship in Organization Studies', *Organization*, vol. 15(1), 5–28.

Alvesson, M. and Due Billing, Y. (1997) *Understanding Gender and Organizations*. London: Sage.

Alvesson, M. and Willmott, H. (2002) 'Identity Regulation as Organizational Control: Producing the Appropriate Individual', *Journal of Management Studies*, vol. 39(5): 619–44.

Anderson, C. J. and Imperia, G. (1992) 'The Corporate Annual Report: A Photo Analysis of Male and Female Portrayals', *The Journal of Business Communication*, vol. 29(2): 113–28.

Ashcraft, K. L. (1999) 'Managing Maternity Leave: A Qualitative Analysis of Temporary Executive Succession', *Administrative Science Quarterly*, vol. 44: 240–80.

Ashcraft, K. L. and Mumby, D. K. (2004) *Reworking Gender: A Feminist Communicology of Organization*. Thousand Oaks, CA: Sage.

Avolio, B. J., Gardner, W. L., Walumbwa, F. O., Luthans, F. and May, D. R. (2004) 'Unlocking the Mask: A Look at the Process by which Authentic Leaders Impact Follower Attitudes and Behavior', *The Leadership Quarterly*, vol. 15: 801–23.

Badaracco, J. (2002). *Leading Quietly*, Cambridge, MA: Harvard Business School Press.

Bass, B. (1990) *Bass and Stodgill's Handbook of Leadership*. NY: Free Press.

BBC (06/10/08) *Woman's Hour*. Jane Garvey interviews Professor Jocelyn Bell Burnell DBE.

Beer, M. (1999) 'Leading Learning and Learning to Lead', in J. Conger, G. Spreitzer and E. Lawler (eds), *The Leader's Change Handbook*: 127–61. San Francisco: Jossey-Bass.

Belenky, M. F., Clinchy, B. M., Goldberger, N. R. and Tarule, J. M. (1986) *Women's Ways of Knowing: The Development of Self, Voice, and Mind*. NY: Basic Books.

Bell, E. (2008) *Reading Management and Organization in Film*. Basingstoke: Palgrave Macmillan.

Benschop, Y. and Meihuizen, H. E. (2002) 'Keeping Up Gendered Appearances: Representations of Gender in Financial Annual Reports', *Accounting, Organizations and Society*, vol. 27: 611–36.

Billing, Y. D. and Alvesson, M. (2000) 'Questioning Feminine Leadership', *Gender, Work and Organization*, vol. 7(3): 144–57.

Boyatzis, R. E. (1982) *The Competent Manager: A Model for Effective Performance*. NY: Wiley.

Boyatzis, R. E., Stubbs, E. and Taylor, S. N. (2002) 'Learning Cognitive and Emotional Intelligence Competences Through Graduate Management Education', *Academy of Management Learning and Education*, vol. 1(2): 150–62.

Brah, A. and Hoy, J. (1989) 'Experiential Learning: A New Orthodoxy', in S.W. Weil and I. McGil (eds), *Making Sense of Experiential Learning: Diversity in Theory and Practice*. Milton Keynes: Open University Press.

Brass, D. J. (1985) 'Men's and Women's Networks: A Study of Interaction Patterns and Influence in an Organization', *Academy of Management Journal*, vol. 28(3): 327–43.

Broadbridge, A. and Hearn, G. (2008) 'Gender Management: New Directions in Research and Continuing Patterns in Practice', *British Journal of Management*, March: 538–49.

Brooks, D. and Brooks, L. (1997) *Seven Secrets of Successful Women: Success Strategies of the Women Who Have Made It and How You Can Follow Their Lead*. NY: McGraw Hill.

Bryan, P. and Mavin, S. (2003) 'Women Learning to Become Managers: Learning to Fit In or to Play a Different Game', *Management Learning*, vol. 34(1): 111–34.

Burke, R. J. and Vinnicombe, S. (2006) 'Guest Editorial', *Women in Management Review*, vol. 21(1): 7–9.

Burns, J. M (1978) *Leadership*. NY: Harper and Row.

Butterfield, D. A. and Grinnell, J. P. (1999) '"Re-viewing" Gender, Leadership and Managerial Behaviour: Do Three Decades of Research Tell Us Anything?', in G. N. Powell (ed.), *Handbook of Gender and Work*. Thousand Oaks, CA: Sage.

Calas, M. B. and Smircich, L. (1996) 'The Woman's Point of View: Feminist Approaches to Organisation Studies' in S. R. Clegg, C. Hardy and W. R. Nord (eds), *Handbook of Organization Studies*: 218–57. London: Sage.

Carless, S. A. (1998) 'Gender Differences in Transformational Leadership: An Examination of Superior, Leader, and Subordinate Perspectives', *Sex Roles*, vol. 39: 887–902.

Casey, A. (2005) 'Enhancing Individual and Organizational Learning', *Management Learning*, vol. 36(2): 131–47.

Cockerell, M. (2008) 'The Making of the Iron Lady', BBC News at news.bbc.co.uk, published 8 June 2008.

Coleman, M. (2005a) *Gender and Headship in the Twenty-first Century*. Report summary Nottingham: NCSL.

—— (2005b) *Gender and Headship in the Twenty-first Century*. Full Report Nottingham: NCSL.

Collinson, D. (2003) 'Identities and Insecurities: Selves at Work', *Organization*, vol. 10(3): 527–47.

—— (2005) 'Dialectics of Leadership', *Human Relations*, 58(11): 1419–42.

Collinson, D. L. and Hearn, J. (1996) (eds) *Men as Managers, Managers as Men; Critical Perspectives on Men, Masculinities and Managements*. London: Sage.

Conger, J. (1998) 'Qualitative Research as the Cornerstone Methodology for Understanding Leadership', *Leadership Quarterly*, vol. 9:(1): 107–21.

Conger, J. and Benjamin, B. (1999*) Building Leaders*. San Fransisco: Jossey Bass.

Conger, J. and Kanungo, R. (1998) *Charismatic Leadership: The Elusive Factor in Organizational Effectiveness*. San Fransisco: Jossey Bass.

Connell, R. (2006) 'Glass Ceilings or Gendered Institutions? Mapping the Gender Regimes of Public Sector Worksites', *Public Administration Review*, November/December: 837–49.

Contu, A. and Wilmott, H., (2003) 'Re-embeding Situatedness: The Importance of Power Relations in Learning Theory', *Organization Science*, vol. 14(3): 283–96.

Daft, R. L. (1998) (revised edn) *Leadership: Theory and Practice*. South western Division: Thomson Learning.

Davies-Netzley, S. A. (1998) 'Women Above the Glass Ceiling: Perceptions on Corporate Mobility and Strategies for Success', *Gender and Society*, vol. 12(3): 339–55.

Day, D. V. (2001) 'Leadership Development: A Review in Context', *Leadership Quarterly*, vol. 11(4): 581–613.

Deal, J. J. (1998) 'Perceptions of Female and Male Managers in the 1990s: Plus Ça Change …', *Sex Roles*, vol. 38: 287–300.

Dellasega, C. (2005) *Mean Girls Grown Up: Adult Women Who are Still Queen Bees, Middle Bees and Afraid-to-Bees*. Wiley Inc.: NJ.

Dougherty, D. and Kunda G. (1991) 'Photography Analysis: A Method to Capture Organisational Belief Systems', in P. Gagliardi (ed.), *Symbols and Artefacts: Views of the Corporate Landscape*. NY: Aldine de Gruyter.

Dundes, L. (2001) 'Disney's Modern Heroine Pocahontas: Revealing Age-old Gender Stereotypes and Role Discontinuity Under a Façade of Liberation', *The Social Science Journal*, vol. 38: 353–65.

Dym, B. and Hutson, H. (2005) *Leadership in Nonprofit Organizations*. London: SAGE.

Eagly, A. H. (2005a) 'Achieving Relational Authenticity in Leadership: Does Gender Matter?' *The Leadership Quarterly*, vol. 16: 459–74.

—— (2005b) 'Has the Managerial Stereotype Become Less Masculine and More Feminine? A Meta-analysis', paper presented at the 14th general meeting of the European Association of Experimental Social Psychology, Würzburg.

Eagly, A. H. and Carli, L. L. (2007) *Through the Labyrinth: The Truth About Women Leaders*. Boston, MA: Harvard Business School Press.

Eagly, A. H. and Johannesen-Schmidt (2001) 'The Leadership Styles of Men and Women', *Journal of Social Issues*, vol. 57: 781–97.

Eagly, A.H. and Johnson, B. (1990) 'Gender and Leadership Style: A Meta-analysis', *Psychological Bulletin*, vol. 108: 233–56.

Eagly, A. H., Makhijani, M. G. and Otto, S. (1991) 'Are Women Evaluated More Favourably than Men', *Psychology of Women Quarterly*, vol. 15: 203–16.

Easterby-Smith, M. and Lyles, M. (2003) *Handbook of Organizational Learning and Knowledge Management*, Oxford: Blackwell.

Elliott, C. and Stead, V. (2008) 'Learning from Leading Women's Experience: Towards a Sociological Understanding', *Leadership*, vol. 4(2): 159–80.

Ellström, P. E. (2001) 'Integrating Learning and Work', *HRDQ*, vol. 12(4): 421–35.

Epstein, C. F. (1991) *Women in Law*, NY: Basic Books.

Equal Opportunities Commission (2007) *Sex and Power: Who Runs Britain?* London: Equal Opportunities Commission.

Equality and Human Rights Commission (2008) *Sex and Power Report*. London: Equality and Human Rights Commission.

Eriksson-Zetterquist, U. and Styhre, A. (2008) 'Overcoming the Glass Barriers: Reflection and Action in the "Women to the Top" Programme', *Gender, Work and Organization*, vol. 15:(2): 133–60.

Erkut, S. (2001) *Inside Women's Power: Learning from Leaders*. Wellesley, MA: Wellesley Center for Women.

Fairhurst, G. T. (2008) 'Discursive Leadership: A Communication Alternative to Leadership Psychology', *Management Communication Quarterly*, vol. 21: 4: 510–21.

Fenstermaker, S. and West, C. (eds) (2002) *Doing Gender, Doing Difference: Inequality, Power and Institutional Change*. NY: Routledge.

Fenwick, T. (2005) 'Ethical Dilemmas of Critical Management Education', *Management Learning*, vol. 36(1): 31–48.

Fiedler, F. E. (1967) *A Theory of Leadership Effectiveness*. NY: McGraw-Hill.

Finger, M. and Buergin Brand, S. (1999) 'The Concept of the Learning Organization Applied to the Transformation of the Public Sector: Conceptual Contributions for Theory Development' in M. Easterby-Smith, J. Burgoyne and L. Araujo (eds), *Organizational Learning and the Learning Organization: Developments in Theory and Practice*. London: Sage.

Fletcher, J. K. (2004) 'The Paradox of Postheroic Leadership: An Essay on Gender, Power, and Transformational Change', *The Leadership Quarterly*, vol. 15: 647–61.

Fook, J. and Gardner, F. (2007) *Practising Critical Reflection: A Resource Handbook*, Berkshire: Open University Press.

Ford, J. (2006) 'Discourses of Leadership: Gender, Identity and Contradiction in a UK Public Sector Organization', *Leadership*, vol. 2(1): 77–99.

Ford, J. and Harding, N. (2007) 'Move over Management: We Are All Leaders Now', *Management Learning*, vol. 38(5): 475–93.

Ford, J., Harding, N and Learmonth, M. (2008). *Leadership as Identity: Constructions and Deconstructions.* Basingstoke: Palgrave Macmillan.

Fox, S. (1997) 'Situated Learning Theory versus Traditional Learning Theory: Why Management Education Should Not Ignore Management Learning', *Systems Practice*, vol. 10(6): 727–47.

Gabriel, Y. (2005) 'MBA and the Education of Leaders: The New Playing Fields of Eton?', *Leadership*, vol. 1(2): 147–63.

Garfinkel, H. (1967) *Studies in Ethnomethodology.* Englewood Cliffs, NJ: Prentice Hall.

Gatrell, C. J. (2005) *Hard Labour: The Sociology of Parenthood.* Maidenhead, Berkshire: Open University Press.

—— (2007a) 'A Fractional Commitment?', *International Journal of Human Resource Management*, vol. 18(3): 462–75.

—— (2007b) 'Secrets and Lies: Breastfeeding and Professional Paid Work', *Social Science and Medicine*, vol. 65: 393–404.

—— (2008) *Embodying Women's Work.* Maidenhead, Berkshire: Open University Press.

Gatrell, C. J. and Cooper, C. (2007) '(No) Cracks in the Glass Ceiling: Women Managers, Stress and the Barriers to Success', in D. Bilimoria and S. K. Piderit (eds), *Handbook on Women in Business and Management*, Cheltenham: Edward Elgar.

Gatrell, C. J. and Swan E., (2008) *Gender and Diversity in Management: A Concise Introduction.* Sage: London

Gherardi, S. and Poggio, B. (2001) 'Creating and Recreating Gender Order in Organizations', *Journal of World Business*, vol. 36(3), 245–59.

—— (2007) 'Tales of Ordinary Leadership', in M. Reynolds and R. Vince (eds), *The Handbook of Experiential Learning and Management Education.* Oxford: Oxford University Press.

Gilligan, C. (1982) *In a Different Voice: Psychological Theory and Women's Development.* Cambridge, MA: Harvard University Press.

Gilman, S. L. (1985) *Difference and Pathology: Stereotypes of Sexuality, Race, and Madness.* Ithaca: Cornell University Press.

Goleman, D. (1996) *Emotional Intelligence: Why It Can Matter More Than IQ.* London: Bloomsbury.

—— (2002) *The New Leaders: Transforming the Art of Leadership into the Science of Results.* London: Little Brown.

Grant Thornton International Business Report, March 2009.

Gray, B. (1994) 'Women-only Management Training' in M. Tanton (ed.), *Women in Management: A Developing Presence*. London: Routledge.

Greenleaf, R. (1977) *Servant Leadership*. San Francisco: Jossey-Bass.

Grint, K. (1997) *Leadership: Classic, Contemporary and Critical Approaches*. Oxford: Oxford University Press.

—— (2000) *The Arts of Leadership*. Oxford: Oxford University Press.

—— (2004) 'Overcoming the Hydra: Leaderless Groups and Terrorism' in Y. Gabriel (ed.), *Myths, Stories and Organizations: Premodern Narratives for Our Times*, Oxford: Oxford University Press.

—— (2005a) 'Problems, Problems, Problems: The Social Construction of "Leadership"', *Human Relations*, vol. 58(11), 1467–94.

—— (2005b) *Leadership Limits and Possibilities*. London: Palgrave Macmillan.

Gubbins, M. C. and Garavan, T. N. (2005) 'Studying HRD Practitioners: A Social Capital Model', *Human Resource Development Review*, vol. 4(2): 189–218.

Guthey, E. and Jackson, B. (2005) 'CEO Portraits and the Authenticity Paradox', *Journal of Management Studies*, vol. 42(5): 1057–82.

Guthey, E., Jackson, B. and Clark, T. (2008) 'Revisualizing Images in Leadership and Organization Studies', paper presented at EIASM Seminar, Said Business School, Oxford.

Hamilton, E. (2006a) 'Whose Story Is It Anyway?' *International Small Business Journal*. vol. 24(3): 253–271.

—— (2006b) 'Entrepreneurial Learning in Family Business', working paper 051, Lancaster University Management School.

Hanson, R. L. (1996) 'A Comparison of Leadership Practices Used by Male and Female Communication Department Chairpersons', *Journal of the Association for Communication Administration*, vol. 1: 40–55.

Hartley J. and Hinksman B. (2003) *Leadership Development: A Systematic Review of the Literature: A Report for the NHS Leadership Centre*. University of Warwick, July.

Hartman, M. S. (ed.) (1999) *Talking Leadership: Conversations with Powerful Women*. New Brunswick: Rutgers University Press.

Heffernan, M. (2004) *The Naked Truth: A Working Woman's Manifesto on Business and What Really Matters*. San Francisco: Jossey-Bass.

Heifetz, R. and Linsky, M. (2002) *Leadership on the Line*, Cambridge MA: Harvard.

Helgesen, S. (1990) *The Female Advantage: Women's Ways of Leadership*. NY: Doubleday.

Heller, R. and Stephens, R. (2005) *The Seven Summits of Success*. Capstone Publishing Ltd: Chichester.

Henke, J. B., Zimmerman, D., and Smith, N. J. (1996) 'Construction of the Female Self: Feminist Readings of the Disney Heroine', *Women's Studies in Communication*, vol. 19: 229–49.

Hersey, P. and Blanchard, K. H. (1982) 'Leadership Style: Attitudes and Behaviors', *Training and Development Journal*, vol. 36(5): 50–2.

Herzfeld, R., Ruderman, M. and Gentry, W. A. (2008) 'The Impact of Gender and Job Level Perceived Career Barriers: The Case of a Dutch Multinational', slide presentation by the *Center for Creative Leadership*.

Hindmarsh, J. H. (1993) 'Tensions and Dichotomies between Theory and Practice: A Study of Alternative Formulations', *International Journal of Lifelong Education*, vol. 12(2): 101–115.

Holmer Nadesan, M. and Trethewey, A. (2000) 'Performing the Enterprising Subject: Gendered Strategies for Success (?)', *Text and Performance Quarterly*, vol. 20(3): 223–50.

Hosking, D. M. (1997) 'Organizing, Leadership, and Skilful Process' in Grint, K. (ed.), *Leadership: Classical, Contemporary and Critical Approaches*, Oxford: Oxford University Press.

Houlihan, M. (2005) 'Reviews: A Manager's Guide to Leadership', *Management Learning*, vol. 36(2): 268–70.

House, R. J. (1971) 'A Path-goal Theory of Leader Effectiveness', *Administrative Science Quarterly*, 16: 321–39.

House, R. J. and Mitchell, T. R. (1974) 'Path-goal Theory of Leadership', *Contemporary Business*, 3(Fall): 81–98.

Hughes, C. (2000) 'Painting New (feminist) Pictures of Human Resource Development (and) Identifying Research Issues for Political Change', *Management Learning*, vol. 31(1): 51–65.

—— (2002) *Women's Contemporary Lives*. London: Routledge.

Hughes, J., Jewson, N. and Unwin, L. (2006) (eds) *Communities of Practice: Critical Perspectives*. London: Routledge.

Ibarra, H. (1992) 'Homophily and Differential Returns: Sex Differences in Network Structure and Access in an Advertising Firm', *Administrative Science Quarterly*, vol. 37(3): 327–43.

—— (1997) 'Paving an Alternative Route: Gender Differences in Managerial Networks', *Social Psychology Quarterly*, vol. 17(2): 257–64.

Iles, P. and Preece, D. (2006) 'Developing Leaders or Developing Leadership? The Academy of Chief Executives' Programmes in the North East of England', *Leadership*, vol. 2(3): 317–40.

Indvik, J.and Northouse, P. (2003) 'Women and Leadership', in P. G. Northouse (ed.), *Leadership: Theory and Practice*. London: Sage.

James, A. (1998) 'Mary, Mary Quite Contrary, How Do Women Leaders Grow?', *Women in Management Review*, vol. 13(2): 67–71.

James, K. T. and Arroba, T. (2005) 'Reading and Carrying: A Framework for Learning about Emotion and Emotionality in Organizational Systems as a Core Aspect of Leadership Development'. *Management Learning*, vol. 36(3): 299–316.

Judge, E (2003) 'Women on Board: Help or hindrance?', *Times*, 11 November: 21.

Kanter, R.M. (1977) *Men and Women of the Corporation*. NY: Basic Books.

Kempster, S. (2006) 'Leadership Learning through Lived Experience: A Process of Apprenticeship?', *Journal of Management and Organisation*, vol. 12: 4–22.

—— (2009) *How Managers Have Learnt to Lead: Exploring the Development of Leadership Practices*. Basingstoke: Palgrave Macmillan.

Kelloway, E. and Barling, J. (2000) 'What Have We Learned about Developing Transformational Leaders?', *Leadership and Organizational Development Journal*, vol. 21: 355–62.

Khuruna, R. (2003) *Searching for a Corporate Saviour: The Irrational Quest for Charismatic CEOs*. Princeton, NJ: Princeton University Press.

Klenke, K. (1999) Women Leaders and Women Managers in the Global Community, *Career Development International*, vol. 4(3): 134–9.

Kinnock, G. and Millar, F. (eds.), *By Faith and Daring*. London: Virago.

Knights, D. and Kerfoot, D. (2004) 'Between Representation and Subjectivity: Gender Binaries and the Politics of Organizational Transformation', *Organization*, vol. 11(4): 430–54.

Kray, L. J. and Thompson, L. (2005) 'Gender Stereotypes and Negotiation Performance: An Examination of Theory and Practice', in B. M. Staw and R. M. Kramer (eds), *Research in Organizational Behaviour: An Annual Series of Analytical Essays and Critical Reviews*, vol. 26, Elsevier.

Kuchinke, K. P. (2005) 'The Self at Work: Theories of Persons, Meaning of Work and Their Implications for HRD', in C. Elliott and S. Turnbull (eds), *Critical Thinking in Human Resource Development*. London: Routledge.

Lamsa, A-M. and Sintonen, T. (2001) 'A Discursive Approach to Understanding Women Leaders in Working Life', *Journal of Business Ethics*, vol. 34(3/4): 255–67.

Lave, J. and Wenger, E. (1991) *Situated Learning: Legitimate Peripheral Participation*. Cambridge: Cambridge University Press.

Levinson, D. J. (1996) *The Seasons of a Woman's Life*. NY: Ballantine Books.

Lipman Blumen, J. (1996) *The Connective Edge*. San Francisco: Jossey-Bass.

—— (2000) 'Connective Leadership', *National College for School Leadership*. Oxford: Oxford University Press.

Manz, C. and Sims, H. P. (1992) 'Becoming a Super-leader', in R. Glaser (ed.), *Classic Readings in Self-managing Teamwork*, King of Prussia, PA: Organisation Design and Development Inc.

Marshall, J. (1984) *Women Managers: Travellers in a Male World*, Chichester: John Wiley.

Marsick, V. J. and Watkins, K. E. (1997) 'Lessons from Informal and Incidental Learning', in *Management Learning: Integrating Perspectives in Theory and Practice*, J. Burgoyne and M. Reynolds(eds), London: Sage.

Martin, J. (1990) 'Deconstructing Organizational Taboos: The Suppression of Gender Conflict in Organizations', *Organization Science*, vol. 1: 339–359.

Martin, P. Y. (1996) 'Gendering and Evaluating Dynamics: Men, Masculinities and Managements', in D. L. Collinson and J. Hearn (eds), *Men as Managers. Managers as Men: Critical Perspectives on Men, Masculinities and Managements*, 186–209. London: Sage.

—— (2003) 'Gender Practices: Practising Gender at Work', *Gender and Society*, vol. 17: 342–66.

Mavin, S. (2006a) 'Venus Envy: Problematizing Solidarity Behaviour and Queen Bees', *Women in Management Review*, vol. 21(4): 264–76.

—— (2006b) 'Venus Envy 2: Sisterhood, Queen Bees and Female Misogyny in Management', *Women in Management Review*, vol. 21(5): 349–64.

—— (2008) 'Queen Bees, Wannabees and Afraid to Bees: No More "Best Enemies" for Women in Management', *British Journal of Management*, vol. 19: S75–S84.

McCarthy, H. (2004) *Girlfriends in High Places: How Women's Networks are Changing the Workplace.* London: Demos.

Meyerson, D. E. and Fletcher, J. K. (2000) 'A Modest Manifesto for Shattering the Glass Ceiling', *Harvard Business Review*, January–February: 127–36.

Miller, L. and Neathy, F. (2004) *Advancing Women in the Workplace: Case Studies*, Manchester: Equal Opportunities Commission.

Mitchell, W. J. T. (1984) 'What Is an Image?', *New Literary History*, vol. 15(3): 503–37.

—— (2005) *What do Pictures Want?* Chicago: The University of Chicago Press.

Moore, G. (1988). 'Women in Elite Positions: Insiders or Outsiders?', *Sociological Forum,* vol. 3: 566–85.

Morrell, K. and Hartley, J. (2006) 'A Model of Political Leadership', *Human Relations*, vol. 59(4): 483–504.

Muijs, D. and Harris, A. (2003) Teacher Leadership – Improvement through Empowerment Educational Management, Administration and Leadership, vol. 31(4): 437–88.

Nahapiet, J. and Ghoshal, S. (1998) 'Social Capital, Intellectual Capital and the Organisational Advantage', *Academy of Management Review*, vol. 23(2): 242–66.

Northouse, P. G. (2004) (3rd ed.) *Leadership: Theory and Practice.* London: Sage.

Olsson S. (2002) 'Gendered Heroes: Male and Female Representations of Executive Identity', *Women in Management Review*, vol. 17: 142–51.

Parry, K. and Hansen, H. (2007) 'The Organizational Story as Leadership', *Leadership*, vol. 3(2): 281–300.

Pearce, C. L. and Conger J. A. (2003) *Shared Leadership: Reframing the Hows and Whys of Leadership.* CA: Sage.

Pedler, M., Burgoyne, J. and Boydell, T. (2004) *A Manager's Guide to Leadership.* London: McGraw-Hill.

Perriton, L. (2006) 'Does Woman + a Network = Career Progression?', *Leadership*, vol. 2(1): 101–13.

Pfeffer, J. (1981) *Power in Organizations.* London: Pitman.

Powell, G. N. and Butterfield, D. A. (2003) 'Gender, Gender Identity and Aspirations to Top Management', *Women in Management Review*, vol. 18, 3/4: 88–96.

Puwar, N. (2004) *Space Invaders: Race, Gender and Bodies Out of Place.* Oxford: Berg Publishers.

Raelin, J. A. (2003) *Creating Leaderful Organizations: How to Bring Out Leadership in Everyone.* NY: Berrett-Koehler.

Reynolds, M. (1997) 'Towards a Critical Management Pedagogy', in J. Burgoyne and M. Reynolds (eds), *Management Learning: Integrative Perspectives in Theory and Practice.* London: Sage.

Rickards, T. and Clark, M. (2006) *Dilemmas of Leadership.* London: Routledge.

Roan, A. and Rooney, D. (2006) 'Shadowing Experiences and the Extension of Communities of Practice: A Case Study of Women Education Managers', *Management Learning*, vol. 37(4): 433–54.

Rodgers, H., Gold, J., Frearson, M. and Holden, R. (2003) 'The Rush to Leadership: Explaining Leadership Development in the Public Sector', working paper Leeds Business School.

Rorty, R. (ed.) (1967) *The Linguistic Turn: Recent Essays in Philosophical Method*. Chicago: University of Chicago Press.

Rosener, J. B. (1990). 'Ways Women Lead', *Harvard Business Review*, vol. 68: 119–25.

Ryan, M. K. and Haslam, S. A. (2005) 'The Glass Cliff: Evidence that Women Are Over-represented in Precarious Leadership Positions', *British Journal of Management*, vol. 16: 81–90.

—— (2007) 'The Glass Cliff: Exploring the Dynamics Surrounding the Appointment of Women to Precarious Leadership Positions', *Academy of Management Review*, vol. 32(2): 549–72.

Salminen-Karlsson, M. (2006) 'Situating Gender in Situated Learning', *Scandinavian Journal of Management*, vol. 22(1): 31–48.

Salvage, J. (2001) 'TV Reputations: Florence Nightingale – Iron Maiden', *BMJ*, vol. 323(7305): 172.

Sarler, C. (13 July 2008) 'Unleashed and Unrepentant: Fleet Street's Bitch Goddesses', *The Independent on Sunday*, UK.

Schein, V. E. (1973) 'The Relationship Between Sex Role Stereotypes and Requisite Management Characteristics', *Journal of Applied Psychology*, vol. 57: 95–105.

—— (1975) 'The Relationship Between Sex Role Stereotypes and Requisite Management Characteristics among Female Managers', *Journal of Applied Psychology*, vol. 60: 340–4.

—— (2001) 'A Global Look at Psychological Barriers to Women's Progress in Management', *Journal of Social Issues*, vol. 57: 675–88.

Shamir, B., Dayan-Horesh, H. and Adler, D. (2005) 'Leading by Biography: Towards a Life-Story Approach to the Study of Leadership', *Leadership*, vol. 1(1): 13–29.

Shamir, B. and Eilam, G. (2005) '"What's Your Story?" A Life-stories Approach to Authentic Leadership Development', *The Leadership Quarterly*, vol. 16: 395–417.

Siebert, S. E., Kraimer, M. L. and Liden, R. C. (2001) ,A Social Capital Theory of Career Success'. *Academy of Management Journal*, vol. 44(2): 219–37.

Simpson, R. and Altman, Y. (2000) 'The Time Bounded Glass Ceiling and Young Women Managers: Career Progress and Career Success – Evidence from the UK', *Journal of European Industrial Training*, 24/2/3/4: 190–8.

Sinclair, A. (2005) *Doing Leadership Differently: Gender, Power and Sexuality in a Changing Business Culture*. Melbourne: Melbourne University Press.

Sinclair, A. and Wilson, V. (2002) *New Faces of Leadership*. Melbourne: Melbourne University Press.

Singh, V., Vinnicombe, S. and Kumra, S. (2006) 'Women in Formal Corporate Networks: An Organizational Citizenship Perspective', *Women in Management Review*, vol. 21(6): 458–82.

Smircich, L. and Morgan, G. (1982) 'Leadership: The Management of Meaning', *Journal of Applied Behavioural Science*, vol. 18(3): 257–73.

Staines, G., Tavis, C. and Jayerante, T. E. (1973) 'The Queen Bee Syndrome', *Psychology Today*, vol. 7(8): 55–60.

Staley, C. C. (1988) 'The Communicative Power of Women Managers: Doubts, Dilemmas, and Management Development Programs' in C. A. Valentine and N. Hoar (eds), *Women and Communicative Power: Theory, Research and Practice*, Annandale, VA: Speech Communication Association.

Stanford, J. H., Oates, B. R. and Flores, D. (1995) 'Women's Leadership Styles: A Heuristic Analysis', *Women in Management Review*, vol. 10(2): 9–16.

Stead, V. (2004) 'Business-focused Evaluation: A Case Study of a Collaborative Model', *HRDI*, vol. 7(1): 39–56.

——— (2005) 'Mentoring: A Model for Leadership Development?', *International Journal of Training and Development*, vol. 9(3): 170–84.

——— (2009) 'A Workshop for Women Leader's Development', working paper for *Leaders for Change*, London: The Health Foundation.

Swan, E. (2005) 'On Bodies, Rhinestones and Pleasures', *Management Learning*, vol. 36(3): 317–33.

——— (2006a), 'Gendered Leadership and Management Development: Therapeutic Cultures at Work' in D. McTavish and K. Miller (eds), *Women in Leadership and Management*. Cheltenham: Edward Elgar.

——— (2006b) *The Missing Pedagogy: Leadership Development, Politics and Social Vision*. Lancaster: CEL.

——— (2007) 'Blue-Eyed Girl? Jane Elliott's Experiential Learning and Anti-Racism' in M. Reynolds and R. Vince (eds), *The Handbook of Experiential Learning and Management Education*. Oxford: Oxford University Press.

Swan, E., Stead, V. and Elliott, C. (2009) 'Research Futures: Women, Diversity and Management Learning', *Management Learning 40th Anniversary Special Issue*.

Tannen, D. (1990). *You Just Don't Understand: Men and Women in Conversation*. NY: Ballantine.

Tannenbaum, R. and Schmidt, W. H. (1973) 'How to Choose a Leadership Pattern', *Harvard Business Review*, vol. 51 (May–June): 162–75.

The Guardian (20 December 2008) 'Nobody Was Safe from Me', Afua Hirsch interviews Baroness Scotland.

The Independent (31 July 2008) 'Women on Top: The Rise of the Female Head'.

The New York Times (3 September 2006) report by D. Leonhardt on The Census.

The Times (13 March 2009) 'Meet the 13 most powerful Muslim women in Britain'.

Timberlake, S. (2005) 'Social Capital and Gender in the Workplace', *The Journal of Management Development*, vol. 24(1): 34–44.

Trethewey, A. (2001) 'Reproducing and Resisting the Master Narrative of Decline: Midlife Professional Women's Experiences of Ageing', *Management Communication Quarterly*, vol. 15: 183–226.

TUC (2008) 'Closing the Gender Pay Gap: An Update Report for TUC Women's Conference 2008'.

Van Maurik, J. (2001) *Writers on Leadership*. London: Penguin Business.

Van Velsor, E., McCauley, C. D. and Moxley, R. S. (1998) 'Our View of Leadership Development' in C. D. McCauley, R. S. Moxley and E.Van Velsor (eds), *The Centre for Creative Leadership Handbook for Leadership Developments* (1st edn), San Fransisco, CA; Jossey Bass.

Vinnicombe, S. (1988) 'What Exactly are the Differences in Male and Female Working Styles?', *Women and Management Review*, 3(1): 13–21.

Vinnicombe, S. and Bank, J. (2003) *Women with Attitude: Lessons for Career Management*. London: Routledge.

Vinnicombe, S., Singh, V. and Kumra, S. (2004) *Making Good Connections: Best Practice for Women's Corporate Networks*, London: Opportunity Now.

Volman, M. and Ten Dam, G. (1998) 'Equal but Different: Contradictions in the Development of Gender Identity in the 1990's', *British Journal of Sociology of Education*, vol. 19(4): 529–45.

Vroom, V. H. and Jago, A. G. (1988) *The New Leadership: Managing Participation in Organizations*. Englewood Cliffs, NJ: Prentice Hall.

Wajcman, J. (1998) *Managing like a Man: Women and Men in Corporate Management*. Cambridge: Polity Press.

West, C. and Fenstermaker, S. (1995) 'Doing Difference', *Gender and Society*, vol. 9: 8–37.

West, C. and Zimmerman, D. H. (1987) 'Doing Gender', *Gender and Society*, vol. 1(2): 125–51.

—— (2005) 'Reading 2: Resources for Doing Gender' in J. West-Burnham (2004) *Building Leadership Capacity – Helping Leaders Learn: An NCSL Thinkpiece*, London: NCSL.

Wharton, A. S. (2005) *The Sociology of Gender: An Introduction to Theory and Research*. MA: Blackwell Publishing.

Wilson, F. (1995) *Organizational Behaviour and Gender*. NY: McGraw Hill.

—— (2003) (2nd revised ed.), *Organizational Behaviour and Gender*, Aldershot: Ashgate Publishing.

Yukl, G. (1999) 'An Evaluative Essay on Current Conceptions of Effective Leadership', *European Journal of Work and Organizational Psychology*, vol. 8(1): 33–48.

—— (2008) (6th ed.) *Leadership in Organisations*. London: Pearson Education.

Index